Picturing Emerson:
An Iconography

Joel Myerson
and
Leslie Perrin Wilson

HOUGHTON LIBRARY

2016

Distributed by Harvard University Press
Cambridge, Massachusetts and London, England

A Special Double Issue of the *Harvard Library Bulletin*
Volume 27: Numbers 1-2

HARVARD LIBRARY BULLETIN
VOLUME 27: NUMBERS 1–2 (SPRING–SUMMER 2016)
PUBLISHED MARCH 2017
ISSN 0017-8136

Editor
William P. Stoneman

Coordinating Editor
Dennis C. Marnon

The Harvard Library Bulletin is published three times a year, by Houghton Library. Annual subscription $35 (U.S., Canada, and Mexico), $41 (foreign); single issue $15; double issue $30.

Editorial correspondence should be addressed to William P. Stoneman, Houghton Library, Harvard University, Cambridge, MA 02138, email stoneman@fas.harvard.edu; claims and subscription inquiries should be addressed to Monique Duhaime, Houghton Library, Harvard University, Cambridge, MA 02138, email duhaime@fas.harvard.edu.

Publication of this special double issue of the Bulletin is made possible by a bequest from George L. Lincoln, Class of 1895, by a fund established in memory of William A. Jackson, and by the Houghton Library Fund to Support the Study of Ralph Waldo Emerson.

The paper used in this publication meets the minimum requirements of the American National Standard for Information Sciences—Permanence of Paper for Printed Materials, ANSI z39.49-1984.

ISBN for this issue is 9780674975972. Distributed by Harvard University Press, Cambridge, Massachusetts and London, England.

To

Ralph H. Orth

Albert J. von Frank

and in memory of

Joyce T. Woodman

Permissions

Images are reproduced by permission of and through the courtesy of Beinecke Rare Book and Manuscript Library, Yale University; Henry W. and Albert A. Berg Collection of English and American Literature, New York Public Library; Boston Athenæum; Bostonian Society; Carlyle House, London; Concord Free Public Library; Concord Museum; George Eastman Museum; Harvard Art Museums; Harvard University Press; Houghton Library; Historic New England; Huntington Library, Art Collections, and Botanical Gardens; Longfellow National Historical Site, Cambridge, Mass.; Joel Myerson Collection of Nineteenth-Century American Literature, Irvin Department of Rare Books and Special Collections, University of South Carolina, Columbia, S.C.; Massachusetts Historical Society; National Library of Sweden; National Portrait Gallery, London; National Portrait Gallery, Washington, D.C.; Pennsylvania Academy of Fine Arts, Philadelphia; and Ralph Waldo Emerson Memorial Association.

The image on the title page is taken from a carte-de-visit of Emerson by William Shew (see page 62).

Contents

Abbreviations

Athenæum	Boston Athenæum
b:	Back (verso) of a carte-de-visite or cabinet card
Berg	Henry W. and Albert A. Berg Collection of English and American Literature, New York Public Library
Bostonian	Bostonian Society, Boston
BPL	Boston Public Library
Bush	Emerson House, Concord
CEC	*The Correspondence of Emerson and Carlyle,* ed. Joseph Slater (New York: Columbia University Press, 1964)
CFPL	Concord Free Public Library
CW	*The Collected Works of Ralph Waldo Emerson*, gen. eds. Alfred R. Ferguson, Joseph Slater, Douglas Emory Wilson, and Ronald A. Bosco, 10 vols. (Cambridge, Mass.: The Belknap Press of Harvard University Press, 1971–2013)
Exhibition	Ronald A. Bosco and Joel Myerson, *Ralph Waldo Emerson: A Bicentennial Exhibition at Houghton Library of the Harvard College Library* (Cambridge, Mass.: Houghton Library, 2003) [also published as the Fall-Winter 2003 double issue of the *Harvard Library Bulletin*]
f:	Front (recto) of a carte-de-visite or cabinet card
f&b:	Front and back (recto and verso) of a carte-de-visite or cabinet card
Facing the Light	Harold Francis Pfister, *Facing the Light: Historic American Daguerreotypes; An Exhibition at the National Portrait Gallery, September 22, 1978–January 15, 1979* (Washington, D.C.: Published for the National Portrait Gallery by the Smithsonian Institution Press, 1978)
HL	Houghton Library, Harvard University
HNE	Historic New England (formerly Society for the Preservation of New England Antiquities)

Ireland   Alexander Ireland, *Ralph Waldo Emerson: His Life, Genius, and Writings*
                 (London: Simpkin, Marshall, 1882)

J   *The Journals of Ralph Waldo Emerson*, ed. Edward Waldo Emerson and
                 Waldo Emerson Forbes, 10 vols. (Boston: Houghton Mifflin, 1909–1914)

JM   Joel Myerson Collection of Nineteenth-Century American Literature,
                 University of South Carolina

JMN   *The Journals and Miscellaneous Notebooks of Ralph Waldo Emerson*,
                 chief eds. William H. Gilman and Ralph H. Orth, 16 vols. (Cambridge,
                 Mass.: The Belknap Press of Harvard University Press, 1960–1982)

L   *The Letters of Ralph Waldo Emerson*, ed. Ralph L. Rusk and Eleanor M.
                 Tilton, 10 vols. (New York: Columbia University Press, 1939–1995)

LetETE   *The Letters of Ellen Tucker Emerson*, ed. Edith E. W. Gregg, 2 vols. (Kent,
                 Ohio: Kent State University Press, 1982)

LetLdE   *The Selected Letters of Lidian Jackson Emerson*, ed. Delores Bird Carpenter
                 (Columbia: University of Missouri Press, 1987)

MHS   Massachusetts Historical Society

OFL   *One First Love: The Letters of Ellen Louisa Tucker to Ralph Waldo Emerson*,
                 ed. Edith W. Gregg (Cambridge, Mass.: Harvard University Press, 1962)

"Portraits"   F. B. Sanborn, "The Portraits of Emerson," *New England Magazine* n.s. 15
                 (December 1896): 449–468

Rusk's notes   Notes compiled by Ralph L. Rusk for his biography of Emerson,
                 Columbia University

Steele and Polito Chris Steele and Ronald Polito, *A Directory of Massachusetts
                 Photographers, 1839–1900* (Camden, Maine: Picton Press, 1993)

von Frank   Albert J. von Frank, *An Emerson Chronology*, 2nd ed., rev. and enl.,
                 2 vols. (Albuquerque, N.Mex.: Studio Non Troppo, 2016)

W   *The Complete Works of Ralph Waldo Emerson*, ed. Edward Waldo
                 Emerson, 12 vols. (Boston and New York: Houghton, Mifflin, 1903–1904)

Ralph Waldo Emerson between 1860 and 1868
by James Wallace Black.

Introduction

Were you ever Daguerrotyped, O immortal man? And did you look with all vigor at the lens of the camera or rather by the direction of the operator at the brass peg a little below it to give the picture the full benefit of your expanded & flashing eye? and in your zeal not to blur the image, did you keep every finger in its place with such energy that your hands became clenched as for fight or despair, & in your resolution to keep your face still, did you feel every muscle becoming every moment more rigid: the brows contracted into a Tartarean frown, and the eyes fixed as they are fixed in a fit, in madness, or in death; and when at last you are relieved of your dismal duties, did you find the curtain drawn perfectly, and the coat perfectly, & the hands true, clenched for combat, and the shape of the face & head? but unhappily the total expression escaped from the face and you held the portrait of a mask instead a man. (*JMN*, 8:115–116)

Ralph Waldo Emerson (May 25, 1803–April 27, 1882) was fascinated by photography from its invention and gave some thought to the processes and results of portraiture—photographic and artistic—about which he made observations in his journals and published writings.[1] He contemplated the superiority of photography over the fine arts for portraiture, saying "I prefer the photograph to any other copy of the living head: the light is the best painter, & makes no mistakes. Truth evermore."[2] Then, too, he saw the capacity of photography to reflect the actual, noting that it was "good for its authenticity," and in this found it distinct from the work of those who expressed themselves in paint or clay. For him, the daguerreotype was "the true Republican style of painting. The Artist stands aside & lets you paint yourself."[3]

---

1   For an excellent discussion of photography and the Transcendentalists, see Sean Ross Meehan, *Mediating American Autobiography: Photography in Emerson, Thoreau, Douglass, and Whitman* (Columbia: University of Missouri Press, 2008); and his essay on "Photography," in *The Oxford Handbook of Transcendentalism*, ed. Joel Myerson et al. (New York: Oxford University Press, 2010), 453–459.

Leslie Perrin Wilson has published two short studies of Emerson images: "'The Tenant is More Than the House': Selected Emerson Portraits in the Concord Free Public Library," *Nineteenth-Century Prose* 33 (Spring 2006): 73–116; and "Portraits," in *Emerson in Context*, ed. Wesley T. Mott (New York: Cambridge University Press, 2014), 233–247.

2   *JMN*, 16:277.

3   *JMN*, 8:106, 142.

Still, Emerson was less enthusiastic about photography when the camera was aimed in his direction. Deeming a great man greater "when he can abolish himself and all heroes, by letting in this element of reason, irrespective of persons . . . into our thought, destroying individualism,"[4] he had difficulty reconciling his own celebrity with his philosophy. In discussing images of himself, he preferred self-denigration: "My portraits . . . generally oscillate between the donkey and the Lothario," claiming that every picture looked "either like a pirate or a zany."[5] He made sweeping generalizations, such as "On the sitter the effect of the Daguerreotypist is asinizing" and "I never find myself in my face,—dislike, almost to pain, every copy or photograph of it that has been taken . . . and must believe that the fault is not in the copies, but in the subject."[6] Unfortunately, he rarely reported on specific, personal reactions to his own studio sittings, even declining to record much information about them in his personal account books, in the keeping of which he was generally meticulous.[7]

Nevertheless, as "the first modern American public intellectual"[8] Emerson could hardly have declined to comply with the demands of publishers, lecture agents, colleagues, and admirers in making himself available to the photographer and the artist. Photography, in particular, defined the popular perception of famous people in the mid-nineteenth century, helping to create public personae. Its early development coincided with the commodification of Emerson as a cultural product. In participating in the process, like it or not, Emerson also contributed to the "ideology of American success" and the "enshrinement of national icons" that was so well represented in the work of Mathew Brady, the premier American portrait photographer of the era.[9] Dozens of photographs were taken of Emerson between the mid-1840s and the early 1880s. While each example of a daguerreotype constituted a unique original, limiting the widespread dissemination of any portrait, once new photographic technologies came along in the 1850s, it became possible to make multiple copies of an image from a single negative, and commercially produced carte-de-visite and cabinet card images of Emerson proliferated.[10] Moreover, engravings and lithographs based on photographs and printed in newspapers and periodicals made the sage's face familiar far and wide.

The sheer quantity of Emerson photographs and their frequent republishing in multiple formats have combined with a number of additional factors to discourage the undertaking

4   *CW*, 4:13–14.

5   Moncure Daniel Conway, *Emerson at Home and Abroad* (Boston: James R. Osgood, 1882), 328; quoted in *LetETE*, 1:465.

6   *JMN*, 9:382; *L*, 6:184.

7   Emerson ultimately gave over responsibility for keeping track of his images to his daughter Ellen (see *L*, 10:185).

8   Lawrence Buell, *Emerson* (Cambridge, Mass.: Harvard University Press, 2003), 9.

9   Alan Trachtenberg, *Reading American Photographs: Images as History, Mathew Brady to Walker Evans* (New York: Hill and Wang, 1989), 38, 43.

10   Cartes-de-visite normally have images mounted on 2½" x 4" card stock and cabinet cards on 4¼" x 6½" cards, although larger cabinet cards were also produced.

of a comprehensive Emerson iconography for the benefit of scholars, curators, collectors, dealers, and others. The lack of such a resource often surprises those seeking specific information—dates, makers, and circumstances of sittings—only to find that it cannot be readily supplied. Given that Emerson was one of the most recognized figures of his time, and that his life is documented in journals, letters, and account books (modern editions of the first two fill thirty volumes), how is it that the answer to a question of dating, for example, often comes in the form of a range of years rather than in a firm four digits?

Very few images of Emerson are dated on photographs or their card mounts, on sketches or paintings, or on plaster or marble busts. Only in rare instances does Emerson describe sitting for a work (although a number of the artists who depicted him wrote about their sessions, but often in ways that conflicted with other accounts) or list the expense in his account books. Moreover, early attempts to date the images of Emerson tended to confuse, not clarify, the issue. Franklin Benjamin Sanborn—a man guilty of a great many textual and biographical offenses, described by one scholar of New England Transcendentalism as the "most officious memorializer" of Concord's authors—muddied the waters of Emerson iconography with the publication in the December 1896 issue of the *New England Magazine* of his "Portraits of Emerson."[11] Sanborn included both photographic and artistic portraits in this treatment, but he was far from comprehensive and in some instances simply inaccurate. In this, he did a disservice to generations of scholars and researchers who, aware that Sanborn had known Emerson personally, trusted him as authoritative.

The faults of Sanborn's anecdotal treatment of the subject were compounded by the Centenary Edition of Emerson's *Works*, published 1903–1904. Edited by Edward Waldo Emerson (Emerson's son, whose expertise regarding his father's portraits might have been assumed), this collected, illustrated edition introduced its own errors of image identification, as did the 1909–1914 edition of Emerson's *Journals*, edited by Edward and his nephew, Waldo Emerson Forbes.[12] Together, Sanborn's article, the Centenary Edition, and the *Journals* were taken as credible sources on Emerson portraiture, but none was as reliable as supposed. In fact, they did not necessarily agree with one another even in their errors, making mistakes and inconsistencies in subsequently published image captions inevitable. Add to this Emerson's own reluctance to leave documentation of his portrait sittings and perhaps also the decline of his popular reputation in the twentieth century, and it is not surprising that scholars, curators, dealers, and collectors have been disinclined to tease out the facts of Emerson iconography.

Sanborn echoed Emerson in expressing dissatisfaction with his portraits: "There are some men, and many women, of whom we never see a satisfactory portrait . . . Emerson

---

11   n.s. 15: 449–468; Lawrence Buell, *The Environmental Imagination: Thoreau, Nature Writing, and the Formation of American Culture* (Cambridge, Mass.: Harvard University Press, 1995), 321–322.

12   Tracking the images of Emerson was made even more confusing by the erratic placement of the inserted plates in various printings of volumes of *Works*, where some volumes contained all the expected plates and other printings of the same volume had different plates or lacked them altogether.

has suffered by this lack of an artist of the higher sort, at the period when his expressive presence could best be portrayed; the sun did him little justice, and those painters and sculptors to whom he sat, though often painstaking and sometimes gifted, had not the art to seize what was most characteristic of the man."[13]

It is true that the face and even the figure of Emerson vary considerably over the surviving body of his portraits (most displaying the public man, but some more personal) generated over seven decades (1820s-1880s). The differences in aspect and affect between them have encouraged a certain wishfulness among stakeholders in Emerson portraiture, a tendency to identify images very likely not of Emerson as depicting him. Indeed, one popular group biography of the 1990s features a cover portrait incorrectly captioned as Emerson.[14] The yearning to discover new Waldos has increased the complexities of Emerson iconography, and—given human nature—will no doubt continue.

The potential uses of an Emerson iconography extend well beyond an immediate need for portraits for illustrative use in publications, documentary films, and other products. Portraiture—and photographic portraiture in particular—provides a personal link to its subject, creating intimate access to character and condition and complementing letters, diaries, and other types of primary documentation as a source of biographical information. Robert D. Richardson Jr.—award-winning author of books on Thoreau, Emerson, and William James—listed as the first of six points for any biographer to remember, "Look at all the pictures you can, especially photographs."[15]

This catalogue was compiled in the hope of partially filling the void created by the absence of a reliable reference source for Emerson portraits. It contains both photographs and works of art (miniatures, silhouettes, pencil drawings, crayon sketches, oil portraits, and sculpture). The compilers (a scholar/collector and a curator) represent two of the richest collections of Emerson portraits in the country, the Joel Myerson Collection of Nineteenth-Century American Literature at the University of South Carolina and the William Munroe Special Collections at the Concord Free Public Library. Both have experienced first-hand the difficulties of providing definitive answers to questions about Emerson images and began work on this iconography to aid in answering queries about images of Emerson.

By design, this is a partial catalogue. Including only portraits produced during Emerson's lifetime, it focuses on those photographs and works of art that might be termed "original" or "non-derivative." Certainly posthumous portraits—which in Emerson's case includes everything from miniature copies of earlier busts to wall paintings on the side of

---

13   "Portraits," 449.

14   See the front dust jacket for Carlos Baker, *Emerson Among the Eccentrics* (New York: Viking, 1996), discussed at length in Appendix A.

15   Robert D. Richardson Jr., "The Perils of Writing Biography," in *Lives Out of Letters: Essays on American Literary Biography and Documentation, in Honor of Robert N. Hudspeth*, ed. Robert D. Habich (Madison, N.J.: Fairleigh Dickinson University Press, 2004), 256.

modern buildings—have a place in the history of reputation and audience.[16] Nevertheless, by their very nature they are either based on more primary lifetime images or simply reflect the interpretive vision of the maker. Removed by at least one degree from Emerson himself, they form their own category, deserving of a separate study, which the compilers sincerely hope someone else will take up. (Since these posthumous portrayals continue to multiply, that task will present its own tribulations.)

In practical terms, the decision to include only lifetime portraits means, for example, that while Daniel Chester French's 1879 bust of Emerson from life is found in these pages, his posthumous and derivative 1914 statue of the seated Emerson in the Concord Free Public Library is not, except insofar as information about it relates to the earlier bust.

Secondly, caricatures—unpublished and published—created during Emerson's lifetime have also been excluded. Alas, this includes Christopher Pearse Cranch's well-known sketch of Emerson as an ambulating eyeball with long legs and top hat and Emerson on horseback, cracking a whip, in Lucius Manlius Sargent's *The Ballad of the Abolition Blunder-buss*.[17] However much such items may actually resemble the sage, they not only were limned at second hand (no sitting subject), but also represent the point of view of the caricaturist more than the appearance of Emerson. It would be misleading to characterize them as true portraits.

Not only do the compilers demonstrate, in this work, that scholarship is a collaborative process, but the history of this project reinforces the point. When he was preparing his 1949 biography of Emerson, Ralph L. Rusk examined all the known images of Emerson then in the hands of family members (mostly at the Emerson house in Concord, called "Bush" by the family since the 1830s) before most of the materials were sent to Houghton Library of Harvard University.[18] Rusk annotated over 14,000 4" x 6" index cards documenting his

---

16   We chose not to trace the reproduction of original images in engravings and similar works unless the reproduction was central to the genealogy of the image. For works that do such comprehensive histories of reception and audience, see Michael J. Deas, *The Portraits and Daguerreotypes of Edgar Allan Poe* (Charlottesville: University Press of Virginia, 1989); Rita K. Gollin, *Portraits of Nathaniel Hawthorne: An Iconography* (DeKalb: Northern Illinois University Press, 1983); John Stauffer et al., *Picturing Frederick Douglass: An Illustrated Biography* (New York: Liveright, 2015); and Mark W. Sullivan, *Picturing Thoreau: Henry David Thoreau and American Visual Culture* (Lanham, Md.: Rowman & Littlefield, 2015).

17   For Cranch's caricatures, see F. DeWolfe Miller, *Christopher Pearse Cranch and His Caricatures of New England Transcendentalism* (Cambridge, Mass.: Harvard University Press, 1951); for Lucius M. Sargent, *The Ballad of the Abolition Blunder-buss* (Boston: n.p., 1861), see Len Gougeon, "Whitman, Emerson, and 'The Ballad of the Abolition Blunder-buss,'" *Walt Whitman Quarterly Review* 3 (Fall 1985): 21–27.

18   Ralph L. Rusk, *The Life of Ralph Waldo Emerson* (New York: Scribners, 1949). Rusk also noted references to pictures when he examined the family materials in preparing his 1939 edition of Emerson's *Letters*. For the transfer of the materials to Harvard, see *Exhibition*, 93–94.

research on Emerson and, before his death in 1956, he gave them to Eleanor M. Tilton to use in preparing her edition of Emerson's letters meant to supplement his. In 1979, Tilton made photocopies of the cards dealing with pictures and mailed them to Myerson.[19]

In the early 1980s, Ralph H. Orth began work on an iconography of Emerson, assembling a ring binder detailing what he had been able to find about images of Emerson in works published through that time, as well as his own visits to libraries holding materials. In the late 1990s, Orth generously gave all his materials to Myerson for use in the present work.

Myerson and Wilson looked through more recent printed materials, did thorough searches of the Internet, and examined as many digital collections of institutions as possible. Not only did we find much more information about known images, but we also discovered some that were previously unknown. And, of course, we discovered some images of "Emerson" that were not, in fact, of him at all.[20]

In the first part of this work, each entry begins with a date (or assumed dates) and a brief description of the image. After the image is reproduced,[21] we offer information, if known, about the occasion on which it was made and the maker(s); comments about it by Emerson, family, and friends; and significant reprintings of it.[22] In the second section following the narrative text for all entries, we provide additional information and locations for the original (in the case of art works or unique photographs) and/or copies (such as cartes-de-visite or cabinet cards). Two appendices discuss apocryphal and unlocated images.

In preparing this iconography, we have had the assistance of the following libraries and librarians: Beinecke Rare Book and Manuscript Library, Yale University (Sara Azam, Melissa Barton); Bodleian Library, Oxford University, John Johnson Collection (Julie Anne Lambert); Boston Athenæum (Patricia Boulos, Stanley Ellis Cushing, Mary Warnement); Boston Public Library (Sean P. Casey, Jane Winton); Bostonian Society (Elizabeth Roscio); Carlyle House, London (Linda Skippings); Concord Museum (Adrienne Donohue, David Wood); the Ralph Waldo Emerson House in Concord (Marie Gordinier); George Eastman Museum, (Ross Knapper); Historic New England, formerly Society for the Preservation of New England Antiquities (Lorna Condon, Jeanne Gamble); Huntington Library, Art

19   These are referenced in the iconography as "Rusk's notes."

20   It is not our purpose to list all the images that are misidentified as being Emerson, only those that have commonly been mistaken as being of him (see Appendix A).

21   In the cases of a secondary image derived from a primary one, such as a head-and-shoulders image cropped from a full-body one, we indicate them with numbers; i.e., (A1) and (A2) are, respectively, the main and secondary images.

22   In quoting from the *JMN*, we have printed the final level of the text and have not reported Emerson's insertions (indicated there by up-and-down arrows [↑↓]) and deletions (indicated there by angle brackets [< >]). For important cancellations in *JMN*, *L*, and the account books, we have lined through the cancelled word (e.g, "~~word~~").

Collections, and Botanical Gardens (Ming Aguilar, Elizabeth Clingerman); Kungliga biblioteket (National Library of Sweden), Stockholm (Karin Sterky); Lincoln Financial Foundation Collection (Adriana Maynard); Massachusetts Historical Society (Anne E. Bentley, Peter Drummey, and Elaine Heavey); National Portrait Gallery, London (Constantia Nicolaides); National Portrait Gallery, Washington, D.C. (Amy Shumard); New York Public Library, Henry W. and Albert A. Berg Collection of English and American Literature and the Prints and Spencer Collections (Isaac Gewirts, Margaret Glover, John Mckeon); Pennsylvania Academy of the Fine Arts (Kyungjoo Ha, Jennifer Johns); and Washington State University (Trevor James Bond). Beatrice Manz graciously gave permission to reproduce and publish an image from the Edith Emerson Forbes and William Hathaway Forbes Papers and Additions at the Massachusetts Historical Society.

We would especially like to thank Leslie A. Morris of Houghton Library, Harvard University, for her usual courtesies in helping us to use the Emerson materials there, and the Ralph Waldo Emerson Memorial Association (Margaret Emerson Bancroft) for granting permission to publish images and documents from Emerson's papers. We also wish to thank the following for various types of assistance: Henry A. Arneth, Ronald A. Bosco, Carina Burman, Catherine Cocks, John Crichton, Gunilla Eklund, Nancy Grayson, Daniel Shealy, and Thomas Wortham.

Joel Myerson would like to thank the following at University of South Carolina: Nina Levine, chair of the English Department for her support of my work; Thomas McNally, Dean of Libraries, for continuing to add to my collection; Michael Weisenburg for digitizing images and commenting on an earlier version of this catalogue; and Elizabeth Sudduth, Director of the Irvin Department of Rare Books and Special Collections, for much assistance in accessing and copying materials. Greta has allowed me to assemble more pictures of Waldo than of her; she is loving, supportive, and forgiving.

Leslie Wilson would like to thank the Concord Free Public Library Corporation—which owns, supports, and manages the holdings of the William Munroe Special Collections—for encouragement in working on this project and Library Director Kerry Cronin for allowing sufficient working time to contribute to it in a meaningful way. Special Collections colleagues Constance Manoli-Skocay, Robert C. W. Hall, and Janaya Kizzie all provided substantive help. And, as always, husband Michael has been unfailingly loyal and positive about my work, despite puzzlement over the potential audience for an Emerson iconography.

As our dedication shows, we owe a great debt to Ralph H. Orth for his pioneering work on the iconography and his generosity in passing it on to Joel Myerson. Albert J. von Frank read through the entire work multiple times and made it much better by sharing his knowledge of Emerson and his times, and especially the information gleaned as he prepared a new edition of his *Emerson Chronology*.[23] And, from the late 1970s until her retirement in

---

23   Albert J. von Frank, *An Emerson Chronology*, 2nd ed., rev. and enl., 2 vols. (Albuquerque, N.Mex.: Studio Non Troppo, 2016).

2005 from the Concord Free Public Library, the late Joyce T. Woodman conscientiously maintained the library's archival photofile. As a member of the Ralph Waldo Emerson Memorial Association, she took particular care in organizing and attempting to identify the CFPL's significant holdings of Emerson and Emerson-related images, revamping the Emerson files to facilitate the celebration of the bicentennial of Emerson's birth in 2003, and frequently expressing frustration that she could not supply makers and dates to most of the photographs. Her good-natured complaints about the problem provided the direct stimulus for Wilson to take up the subject.

We both thank Duncan G. Todd and Dennis C. Marnon for their exemplary work in helping to bring this project to print.

There remains the unalterable fact that just as soon as any type of descriptive catalogue is published, someone will step forward with a hitherto-unseen example of the genre that ought to have been included in it. The compilers would welcome hearing from those who have something to add to this iconography, within its defined scope. For this reason, this work constitutes the opening up of a dialogue—preferably lively—rather than a final word.

Joel Myerson
Carolina Distinguished Professor
of American Literature, Emeritus,
University of South Carolina

Leslie Perrin Wilson
Curator, William Munroe Special
Collections, Concord Free Public Library

Picturing Emerson: An Iconography

1829

Painting of Emerson in 1829 by Sarah Goodridge

Two versions have been located:

(A) *Ambrotype from a painting*   (B)
by Sarah Goodridge.

According to Edith W. Gregg, Sarah Goodridge (1788–1853) painted a now-lost miniature of Emerson (then in his mid-twenties) between January and April 1829. On 26 April, Edward Emerson wrote his brother William "Miniatures of Miss Ellen & Waldo came . . . & are well executed: that of Miss E. is nearly perfect." Image (B) is reproduced in *OFL* after 20, as is one of Ellen; the original of the one of Ellen is at the Concord Museum, and a watercolor on ivory of Ellen, also at the Concord Museum (possibly a copy by Caroline Schetky), is reproduced in color in *Exhibition*, 20, and is probably the "Ellen Tucker pin" to which Emerson's daughter Ellen refers in 1861.

Ellen Louisa Tucker wrote her fiancé in May 1829,

> I paint you often in your study—often in your daily walks—*sometimes* opening the red morroco case [with his picture]—as for me I do not love to look at your miniature—'tis so speechless and says any thing in the world

but—"Nelly I love you"   though were it to utter these words I would not hesitate to say promptly and from my soul   No——"Ellen I regret you" would be fitter much and suit the forboding expression——Who would delight in the motionless ivory when the moving speaking original is yet so freshly before me—and of two pictures I would contemplate the best.

Emerson referred to the miniature of Ellen in a rejected stanza of "Thine Eyes Still Shined": "I need not hide beneath my vest / Thy picture, the pride of art, / For I bear it [three words inserted] thy picture burns within my breast, / And the chain is round my heart."

Sanborn, citing Sarah Alden Bradford Ripley (whose husband was Waldo's uncle) about Emerson's image, commented that "neither Mrs. Emerson nor the children recalled the period when it was a good likeness, if ever it can have been," but "a note on the back of the photograph [image (B)] in E[dward]. W[aldo]. Forbes's handwriting" stated "Mother (Edith Emerson Forbes) says that Grandmother [Lidian Emerson] liked it and said it was perfect of him at the time."

1843

Painted silhouette of Emerson in about 1843

First published in David Greene Haskins, *Ralph Waldo Emerson: His Maternal Ancestors*, where it is described as "Taken about 1843." The dating of this image is based solely on the description in Haskins's book.

1844

Miniatures of Emerson in 1844 painted by Caroline Neagus Hildreth

On 25 May 1844, Emerson wrote Caroline Sturgis about Hildreth (1814–1867), "Will you not . . . ask her to show you my miniature, which she finished yesterday, & see with wonder what a beau I am?" Waldo wrote his brother William on 7 June 1844 that he and his daughter Edith had "sat for our miniatures, which took the best hours of a week, I lament to say . . . . Miss Neagus now Mrs Hildreth asked leave to come here & paint my miniature & after some time she wd. give it to Lidian. L. accepted the proposal. She came & painted, they say, an excellent one, & has carried it off to the artists' gallery. I thought it did me too much honour, nor could I find my haggard self in this rosy young beau" (he was all of thirty-one). Emerson gave fifteen dollars to his sister-in-law for "Mrs. Hildreth" on 10 June 1844, and later account book entries show $10.00 for a "picture frame from Mrs Hildreth" on 9 July; $20.00 for "crayon portraits" of his daughters Ellen and Edith on 19 October; and an unspecified amount for frames for the latter pictures on 6 December.

Emerson sat for another miniature, probably in September: he apologized to Hildreth for being busy with his literary projects and in "this plight, I can not offer myself as a subject to your pencil, I think, sooner than the 15th of September." On 14[?] October he wrote William, "Mrs Hildreth has gone to Boston & carried the new miniature, which divides opinions here somewhat, Mrs H. being sure that she has a better likeness than the old one & some of us consenting whilst the majority prefer the old one. She and all are discontented with the eyes, and I am to sit once more next Thursday for them." About the "new miniature," Emerson wrote William on 3 December 1844 that his neighbor Elizabeth Hoar "did not like the expression," but Hildreth was "sure it is better than the old one, much better, all but the eyes which she will alter at my first visit to Boston. George Bradford, Abel Adams, & Lucia Russell all good authorities say the same thing. The other principal witnesses are on the other side." Emerson sent the second miniature to William on 17 December, saying he "must judge of it." If he wanted it, then Hildreth "reports that on account of the larger size of the ivory she demands 35 dollars for the picture, and that the case costs $5.00. which you can return if you wish to frame it or if you wish to provide yourself with a case of a simpler pattern. If however, you keep the case, you must have it made tight by a piece of gold-beater's skin, to preserve the picture from the air." He added, "I am in some consternation at costing Susan [William's wife] so much but I am very sure that the artist has bestowed unwearied pains on the picture, & Mr Saml Ripley told mother yesterday that it was perfect. If you don't like it, I think you must return it to the painter, & let her copy her first piece which is of a different expression." William sent Waldo $40.00 for the picture but they continued to negotiate on the frame; eventually, Waldo paid Mrs. Hildreth $35.00 for "miniatures" and five dollars for a case on William's behalf.

The image is best known by its reproduction as the frontispiece to *J*, 1, where it is described in the list of illustrations as a "Photogravure" from "a miniature painting, in 1844, by Mrs. Richard Hildreth" (at right).

Sanborn later called it "a pleasing and poetic head, not remarkable for strength."

1846

Daguerreotype of Emerson in 1846 by Alfred Sands Southworth

(A)   (B)

As early as 1841, the British poet John Sterling had asked Thomas Carlyle about obtaining an image of Emerson. Carlyle replied, "There is no likeness of the face of Emerson that I know of; I fancy he never yet was engraved: poor fellow, it lies among his liabilities, to be engraved yet, to become a sect-founder, and go partially to the Devil in several ways,—all which may the kind Heavens forbid!" Emerson himself began writing journal entries about daguerreotypes in 1841, but it was not until 14 May 1846, after Carlyle had asked him for a picture, that he wrote about sending him one: "I was in Boston the other day & went to the best reputed Daguerr[e]otypist, but though I brought home three transcripts of my face, the housemates voted them rueful, supremely ridiculous, I must sit again, or, as true Elizabeth Hoar said, I must not sit again, not being of the right complexion which Daguerre & iodine delight in. I am minded to try once more, and if the sun will not take me, I must sit to a good crayon sketcher," and on the 31st,

> last Monday, which was my forty third birthday, I went to a new
> Daguerr[e]otypist, who took much pains to make his picture right. I brought

Joel Myerson and Leslie Perrin Wilson 13

home three shadows not agreeable to my own eyes. The machine has a
bad effect on me. My wife protests against the imprints as slanderous. My
friends say, they look ten years older, and, as I think, with the air of a decayed
gentleman touched with his first paralysis. However I got yesterday a trusty
vote or two for sending one of them to you, on the ground that I am not likely
to get a better.

A studio ledger confirms that Emerson visited Southworth and Hawes on 25 May.

Later, in June, Emerson declined having a new daguerreotype made because he felt
himself "a very bad subject for that style."

Carlyle commented to Emerson on "the Photograph" on 17 July:

> . . . this poor Shadow, it is all you could do at present in that matter! But it
> must not rest there, no. This Image is altogether unsatisfactory, illusive, and
> even in some measure tragical to me! First of all, it is a bad Photograph;
> no eyes discernible, at least one of the eyes not, except in rare favourable
> lights: then, alas, Time itself and Oblivion must have been busy. I could
> not at first, nor can I yet with perfect decisiveness, bring out any feature
> completely recalling to me the old Emerson, that lighted on us from the
> Blue, at Craigenputtock, long ago,—eheu! Here is a genial, smiling energetic
> face, full of sunny strength, intelligence, integrity, good humour; but it lies
> imprisoned in baleful shades, as of the valley of Death; seems smiling on me
> as if in mockery, "Dost know me, friend? I am dead, thou seest, and distant,
> and forever hidden from thee;—I belong already to the Eternities, and thou
> recognisest me not!" On the whole, it is the strangest feeling I have:—and
> practically the thing will be that you get us by the earliest opportunity some
> living pictorial sketch, chalk-drawing or the like, from a trustworthy hand;
> and send it hither to represent you. Out of the two I shall compile for myself
> a likeness by degrees: but as for this present, we cannot put up with it at all; to
> my Wife and me, and to sundry other parties far and near that have interest in
> it, there is no satisfaction in this.

The 1846 daguerreotype may be the one Bronson Alcott refers to in a 19 February 1850
journal entry: "I tried the other day to persuade E. to sit at Southworth's, for a daguerreotype,
but he declined, saying that Southworth's impressions had been failures hitherto, & did not
please him."

Alexander Ireland, who helped Emerson with his British lecture tours, told Carlyle
in March 1847 that he "professed to know [Emerson] by the photograph," which, Carlyle
added, "I never yet can." In his 1882 biography of Emerson, Ireland reproduced the image
below (pasted in the book) as "from a daguerreotype taken while he was in England, in 1847
. . . His own family regard this likeness as the best, at this period of his life."

ÆT. 44.

1846

Crayon and chalk portrait of Emerson in the fall of 1846 by Eastman Johnson

Although according to Margaret C. S. Christman, Emerson "complied with Henry Wadsworth Longfellow's request that he sit for his portrait on October 22 [1846], just after he had returned from a fortnight in Bangor, Maine," in their study of the painter, Teresa A. Carbone and Patricia Hills state that "the exact timing of [Emerson's] own sittings with Johnson is unclear." In the "List of Illustrations" in *J*, 5, this is dated "about 1846."

Longfellow sat for Johnson (1824–1906), who had moved to Washington a year or two before and became known for his crayon portraits, in September 1846. He then commissioned Johnson to prepare a series of portraits of his friends. Sanborn considered this "the poorest" of the three crayon sketches done of Emerson.

About a year before his death, Johnson recollected the sitting: "No one ever impressed me so as being a perfectly spiritual man, in mind, in appearance, and manner. His aspect was gentle and lovely, his talk like an angel—oh, every look, every word, every action, was as beautiful as could be conceived. I never met any man like him in that respect. I remember him just as well as if it were a week ago. His beautiful smile—he was a lovely man to be near to. He was a perfect saint—better than that."

1848

Daguerreotype of Emerson in 1848

First published (partially and identified as Emerson) in Townsend Scudder, *The Lonely Wayfaring Man: Emerson and Some Englishmen*, and described as a daguerreotype taken in Liverpool in 1848.

The daguerreotype is housed at the Beinecke Library at Yale with a note that reads "Ralph Waldo Emerson at the age of 46. Presented by Emerson to Miss Neuberg, sister of Joseph Neuberg of Nottingham England, Carlyle's secretary and friend. Given in 1914 by F. J. Frankau, Miss Neuberg's (Mrs. Frankau's) son, of London England, to Eliza Brush Pirsson, to go to the Yale University Library."

Emerson stayed with Joseph Neuberg in Nottingham in December 1847, lecturing there on the sixth and eighth, and Pirsson's notes on this picture state that Emerson "gave this portrait to Miss Neuberg, the young and attractive sister of his host," while "a guest in the family." When Emerson met Neuberg's sister Rosette or Rosetta Neuberg, he was surprised that their acquaintance with Carlyle was confined to writings: "I do believe my brother would give his little finger to <u>know</u> Carlyle," she told him, and Emerson replied, "I shall not leave England without bringing the two together," which he did in the spring of 1848.

Joel Myerson and Leslie Perrin Wilson 17

1848

Oil painting of Emerson in 1848 by David Scott

This portrait of Emerson at about forty-five in the lecture stance—with the characteristic clenched fist—was painted during Emerson's second trip abroad.

Artist David Scott (1806–1849) was a transatlantic admirer of Emerson's work before the two met. They were introduced at the Edinburgh home of Dr. Samuel Brown in February 1848. Scott was eager to paint Emerson and invited him to breakfast. In a letter to his wife, Emerson described the artist as "a sort of Bronson Alcott with easel & brushes," a "sincere great man, grave, silent, contemplative & plain," and a "noble stoic sitting apart here among his rainbow allegories, very much respected by all superior persons." Emerson sat for Scott at the artist's studio outside Edinburgh. Scott worked to overcome Emerson's natural reserve— he found Emerson "guarded, and somewhat cold at times," and his appearance "severe, and dry, and hard." In striving to capture Emerson in the act of communication, he hoped to bring out the personality of his subject. He also suggested Emerson's Transcendental optimism through the symbolic rainbow in the upper left corner of the painting.

According to Bronson Alcott, writing in 1850, the British publisher John Chapman had wished to use this image in a new edition of Emerson's *Poems* (1847); however, the second printing in 1850 was done by George Routledge.

Scott died at forty-three, the year after he painted Emerson. In 1869, his brother William Bell Scott sent the portrait to the United States, and William J. Linton, acting for him, offered to sell it for $1,000, but offered to reduce the price to $700 if Emerson or any of his friends wished to buy it before the public offering. Emerson replied on 21 September that neither his wife nor his children (Edward and Ellen) had seen it, but would go to Boston to examine the picture, though he warned, "'Tis very certain we shall never buy it as we have no money to spend for our own images." Ultimately, Emerson's friend Judge Ebenezer Rockwood Hoar, Hoar's sister Elizabeth (fiancée of Emerson's brother Charles, who died in 1836), and Reuben N. Rice (an original member of the library committee for the CFPL) purchased the painting for donation to Concord's newly founded library in 1873. It now hangs in the reference room of the CFPL.

The critical assessment of the portrait by Edward Emerson, himself an amateur painter, was tempered by his admiration for its symbolism: "David Scott . . . has this one merit in that wooden picture that he made of my father, in that he recognized that my father stood for Hope, and he put the rainbow in the background—the symbol of hope." Moncure Daniel Conway found the Scott portrait "a very successful rendering of the peculiarities of Emerson's look and manner" and asserted that it captured "characteristics photographed on the mind of one who has attentively listened to Emerson." Sanborn pronounced it the "best of his [Emerson's] portraits . . . since it well preserves the orator's attitude," but he also described it as "rather hard and cold in color" and noted that "the coloring is too dark." A reproduction was used as the frontispiece in *W*, 5.

1848[?]

Photograph of Emerson in 1848[?]

First published in *CEC*, where it is dated "1848." No further information is known.

1850s[?]

Drawings of Emerson by Harriot Appleton Curtis

Written on the back of the images is "Three original pencil sketches of R. W. Emerson by Miss Harriot Appleton." The third image is definitely not Emerson. No further information is known.

Harriot Sumner Appleton Curtis (1841–1923) was the daughter of Nathan Appleton, a prominent Boston politician and businessman who was the father of Henry Wadsworth Longfellow's second wife, Fanny. Dated by HNE "1850–1860." The broad-brimmed hat is typical of one worn by Emerson.

1850

Drawing of Emerson in 1850 by Fredrika Bremer

The accounts by Fredrika Bremer (1801–1865), a Swedish author and advocate for feminist causes, of her meetings with Emerson were published in *America of the Fifties: Letters of Fredrika Bremer*. Signe Alice Rooth's *Seeress of the Northland: Fredrika Bremer's American Journey, 1849–1851* includes further information about this trip. Emerson mentions her visits to Concord in his letters of 3 December 1849, 17 January 1850, and 10 August 1851; he also met her in New York on 16 March 1850. Bronson Alcott wrote in his journal on 1 January 1850 after meeting Bremer: "Her talent for drawing came out quite unexpectedly in some pencil sketches which she showed me . . . I thought these pictures were quite characteristic & delicately drawn." In England, George Eliot, in a letter of 19 October 1851, commented on seeing Bremer's "portrait of Emerson, marvellously like."

Joel Myerson and Leslie Perrin Wilson 21

1854

Daguerreotypes of Emerson in 1854 by Josiah Johnson Hawes

Two versions have been noted:

(A1)

Dated on the basis of the May 1903 *New England Magazine* ("From a daguerreotype, in the possession of the family, taken by Hawes in 1854"), the frontispiece dated 1854 in *The Centenary of the Birth of Ralph Waldo Emerson*, and the "List of Illustrations" in *W*, 2 ("from a daguerreotype taken by Hawes in 1854, now in the possession of the family, and never before reproduced"). Hawes (1808–1891) formed a partnership in 1843 with Albert Southworth (1811–1894) that became one of the most prestigious Boston photographic studios.

This may be one of the "Daguerreotypes" Ellen Emerson asked her mother to send her on 19 February 1854. The date of autumn 1856 is ascribed by Rufus Rockwell Wilson.

This image served as the basis for an engraving by Leopold Grozelier (1830–1865). On 20 November 1856, William Lloyd Garrison wrote Emerson about how the author and lecturer Charles Henry Brainard (1817–1885) was planning to publish "'a magnificent lithographic print' . . . in which will be presented the portraits, drawn from daguerreotypes taken expressly for the purpose, of Theodore Parker, Wendell Phillips, Joshua R. Giddings, Gerrit Smith, Samuel J. May, &c.," and he asked, on Brainard's behalf, "whether you are willing to allow him to put your likeness among the others; and, if so, whether you have a good daguerreotype portrait of yourself, which you would kindly permit the artist to copy from . . . . Should you consent, and yet have no satisfactory likeness of yourself, should you visit the city in the course of a fortnight, arrangements can be made for a sitting to one of our best daguerreotypists." Emerson replied on 5 December that he would comply, "though I am a very bad sitter to the Daguerre artists." His image was included with the others in the 1857 broadside print *Heralds of Freedom*, which was advertised as "this day published" in the 9 January 1857 *Liberator*, priced at $1.50:

Collection of the Massachusetts Historical Society

Grozelier was a French-born artist and engraver who married the artist Sara Peters in 1855. Because the *Liberator* advertisement noted that copies were for sale at Brainard's and at the *Liberator* offices, this broadside may have been used as a fundraiser for Garrison's paper, which would explain his involvement.

Joel Myerson and Leslie Perrin Wilson 23

Ralph Waldo Emerson
1854

(A2)

Reproduced in reverse in Mary Miller Engel, *I Remember the Emersons*. Engel states that in approximately 1902 Edward Waldo Emerson gifted her "the photograph of his father that he considered the best one of him, one taken in 1854," which is the one reproduced in her book. Edward may have given her this picture when he was choosing a version of it for inclusion in *W*, 2.

(B)

Ellen Emerson, writing on 2 March 1868 to Gisela von Arnim Grimm in Germany, responding to her request for photographs, mentioned, among others,

> a large photograph, taken fifteen years ago [ca. 1853], which we contemptuously discarded, though the photographer said to Mother and me "A man's family are

no judges of how he appears to the public. This may not be the Father, but it is the orator, the man as he stands before the world, and this will be the one picture valued by posterity, when all the others are forgotten." I was struck by what he said, and remembered it. We kept one copy of the head, but I never have seen it elsewhere during the whole fifteen years. But within three months somebody has discovered it in Southworth & Hawes shop, dragg[e]d it from obscurity, made Hawes make many copies, and it is admired and eagerly sought for, all Father's friends fulfilling Southworth's prophecy of fifteen years since. I will send you that.

Emerson seemed to like this image. Writing Anne Charlotte Lynch Botta on 24 February 1868, he enclosed what was probably this picture, to which she responded on 13 April, "I have delayed acknowledging . . . the very excellent photograph . . . . I thank you very much for the picture; it seems to me to convey a better idea of the 'real presence' than any I have seen of you. The other which you promise I shall hope you will bring when you make to me the long-expected visit." Also in 1868, Emerson sent another "one of Southworths" to Annie Downs. The next year he wrote another friend on 24 January that he was "carrying" with him "the Southworth head" for his next visit. As late as 14 December 1871 he noted in his journal that he wished to send "Southworth's large photograph" to two friends in Chicago.

Sanborn wrote that the two daguerreotypes by Southworth and Hawes studio are among the best of the many pictures of Emerson made after 1850 (the other is probably image [B] from 1858[?]; see pages 29–30). In his 1882 biography of Emerson, Alexander Ireland reproduced image (B), pasted in the book, as "reduced from a large one which he sent to the author in 1867, probably taken a few years before." Also in 1882, Bronson Alcott used this image as the frontispiece to his *Ralph Waldo Emerson*. It appears in James Elliot Cabot's *A Memoir of Ralph Waldo Emerson* as an engraving by Dr. William Herbert Rollins after a "well-known" photograph by Hawes "made, Mr. Hawes thinks, in 1856: the best likeness that we have of Emerson, as it appears to me." But Frederic Henry Hedge, an old friend of Emerson's, regretted that Cabot chose for his frontispiece

a "counterfeit presentment" of Emerson which shows him much darker than his actual complexion. One would judge from this portrait that his hair was black, whereas it was nearer blond than black, and that the impression of his countenance was sombre instead of fair and radiant, as he appeared in society. But this portrait, if it gives a false impression, preserves what is not less important, the physiognomical character of his visage. . . . I once came upon Emerson while he was sleeping, and was startled at the stern character of a face which I had known only as radiant and inviting.

Also reproduced as the frontispiece to *W*, 9, where it is dated "1854."

MID-1850S

Emerson in the mid-1850s

Three versions have been noted:

No further information is known.

(A)

(B)

(C)

1857[?] AND 1858[?]

Daguerreotypes of Emerson in 1857[?] and 1858[?] by Southworth and Hawes

Three versions have been noted:

(A) 1857[?]

First published in Robert A. Sobieszek, *The Spirit of Fact*, where it is assigned a date of 1857. In *Facing the Light*, Pfister comments "Emerson appears not to have aged dramatically before 1858–59." Considering that Southworth and Hawes were making appointments for him as early as 1849, a date in the early 1850s would not be impossible or unreasonable.

(B1) 1858[?]

Image (B1) is a photograph of the daguerreotype without its case and image (B2) shows its present state. The daguerreotype was probably taken from its case when it was used in *Facing the Light*, 141.

Joel Myerson and Leslie Perrin Wilson 29

(B2) 1858[?]

Sanborn believed this image was not "faithful to the serious expression of the thinker, but may serve to recall some lively moments of playful conversation, when thought gave place to fun."

HL dates this as "ca. 1848," states it is "possibly" by Southworth and Hawes; it is inscribed on back: "Mr. Grozelier / 7 Montgomery St. / 1858." The HL daguerreotype is reproduced in color in *Exhibition*, facing 1. Both *Literature & Photography*, ed. Jane M. Rabb, and Melissa Banta, *A Curious & Ingenious Art*, misdate this image as the one that Emerson sent Carlyle in 1846. It is dated "ca. 1850" in *Facing the Light*.

First reproduced in 1887 on the title page of David Greene Haskins, *Ralph Waldo Emerson: His Maternal Ancestors*. Reproduced in *W*, 3, and described in the "List of Illustrations" as "From a daguerreotype taken in 1859, in the possession of the family," but, when reproduced in *W*, 6, the table of contents states "From a daguerreotype taken by John A. Whipple of Boston, in 1859, and is now first reproduced through the courtesy of Mrs. L. P. Grozelier," wife of Leopold Grozelier. See *Note One* below.

Note one: This image is best known through a lithograph by Leopold Grozelier (copyright 1859):

The size of the image in the framed engraving at Bush is 22¼" x 16½", and is inscribed by Grozelier.

A popular image, it was advertised as late as 1890 as one "especially liked by the Emerson family." The 31" x 24" poster ("Only a few copies now remain") was offered for $1.50.

Note two: The attributions of the image to both Whipple (1822–1891), an inventor who pioneered night and astronomic photography, and fellow photographer James Wallace Black (1825–1896) is not surprising: they were partners between 1856 and 1859. Black, rather than Whipple, may have continued making copies of the image: he was at 333 Washington Street between 1875 and 1901.

1858

Crayon sketches of Emerson in 1858 by Samuel Worcester Rowse

Two versions have been noted:

(A)

Emerson wrote in his journal between 11 May and 8 June 1858: "Rowse said that a portrait should be made by a few continuous strokes giving the great lines, but if made by labor & by many corrections, though it became at last accurate, it would give an artist no pleasure,— would look muddy. Any body could make a likeness by main strength." And in a letter of 19 July 1858, he wrote, "I think nothing can be done at present with Mr Rowse's sketch. He left it imperfect six weeks ago, not being contented with its progress & intending, I believe, to try to mend it, after an interval, or to make a new one." Rowse (1822–1901) was an illustrator and painter.

There are a number of accounts of this sitting. Ellen Emerson, on 7 May, felt the "picture is, so far, the best that has been made," but on the eleventh she felt Rowse "has spoilt his picture and gone away to give Father a rest before he tries again." Sanborn stated that Rowse "threw aside" the sketch because he believed it had "some defect of drawing," but "it pleased Mrs. Emerson so much that she copied it, and she also allowed me to have it photographed [but see Waldo's account book entry, below, for who paid for these]. Three copies were then printed, one of which I sent to a friend in Germany, for Herman Grimm, an admirer of Emerson, one to my mother in New Hampshire, and the third I retained. From this, somewhat faded, photographs were made for Mr. Alcott's own illustrated book of sonnets, in 1882," and which was the one reproduced by Sanborn. When it was included in W, 6, the "List of Illustrations" stated: "From a photograph in the possession of the family, made from the first crayon drawn in 1857, by S. W. Rowse. The artist made a second drawing, also reproduced in this volume, and then destroyed the first, with which he was not satisfied."

On 12 November 1858, Emerson entered into his account book "Pd S. W. Rowse for 3 photographs to be procured from his first sketch 5.00."

Years later, Edward Waldo Emerson commented:

> Rowse, commissioned by Mr. [Charles Eliot] Norton to draw Emerson's head, is domiciled at his home in Concord . . . . The portrait prospered, had a pleasing freedom in the handling, an open-air look. But one morning Rowse got up early and endeavoured to make some little improvement. When the family came down to breakfast he told them that the meddling had been fatal, and he must begin again. The picture was probably destroyed by him, but fortunately a small photograph was taken at Mrs. Emerson's request . . . . The new picture pleased Mr. Norton. He wrote in a letter after Rowse's death . . . "To those who did not know him personally his name is likely to recall the draughtsman of the best portrait of Emerson."

Edward thought Rowse's sketches "though a little deficient in strength . . . pleasing and good," and that "Rowse's crayon, which always hung at Shady Hill [Norton's home], is a good likeness, but tightly drawn and with a weak mouth." Sanborn considered this sketch had "a certain nobility of expression," and he continued, "What has always pleased me in this Rowse sketch is the lofty air of cheerful courage and hospitality, so native to Emerson, yet so hard for his photographers and painters to reproduce. It was an expression so constant, and yet so inward and fleeting to the eye of sense (apparently), that it was apt to be caricatured, as in the finished crayon of Rowse, where the smile degenerates almost to a simper."

(B)

The Boston correspondent "F." of the December 1858 *Crayon* stated that "At Williams and Everett's is to be seen Mr. Rowse's admirable crayon portrait of Ralph Waldo Emerson, which adds not a little to the already high reputation of the artist. Mr. [Samuel] Masury, the photographer, has taken from the drawing a photograph so uncommonly good, that it is said by critics to be 'even better than the original,' if such a thing were possible." The artist William James Stillman, who himself later painted Emerson (see 1858), believed the Williams and Everett reproduction "one of the most masterly and subtile records of the character of a signal man, nay, the most masterly, we have ever seen. Those who know Emerson best will recognize him most fully in it. It represents him in his most characteristic mood, the subtile intelligence mingling with the kindly humor in his face, thoughtful, cordial, philosophic.

The portrait is not more happy in the comprehension of character than in the rendering of it, and is as masterly technically as it is grandly characteristic."

Lidian Emerson, writing on 11 May 1861 about Thomas Ridgeway Gould's bust of Emerson (see 1861), said, "This bust will refute to posterity, some of the slander going round about him [Emerson] in the form of photographs &c.—not excepting Rowse's last."

Emerson sent a copy of this image to his brother William in January 1859 and another copy to Anne Charlotte Lynch Botta on 29 December 1865, along with "another, after nature, far less respectable." The British poet Arthur Hugh Clough probably commented on this image when he wrote to Charles Eliot Norton that it is "I think without any question the best portrait of any living and known-to-me man that I have ever seen," adding that when he showed to it James Anthony Froude, he, too, "was equally struck by it." Charles J. Woodbury, who first met Emerson in about 1865, felt the Rowse portrait "reproduced the large featuring of his face, with that wise, determined nose (called straight, like the Damascus road) which other Emersons have, and the tender, shrewd eyes, that until the very end kept so much sunshine in them." But Ednah Dow Cheney remembered showing a "photograph" of the Rowse portrait to Theodore Parker, who remarked, "That is not Emerson; that man could not do the things Emerson has done."

Note: An engraving of image (B) by Stephen Alonzo Schoff, the more widely reproduced of the Rowse images, first appeared (dated "1857") in *The Correspondence of Thomas Carlyle and Ralph Waldo Emerson*:

About this image, Edward Waldo Emerson said "Schoff has improved his etching and will, I think, still more improve it." George William Curtis considered this "a remarkable and beautiful specimen," the "finest and most satisfactory portrait of Emerson that we shall ever have." But another of Emerson's friends, Frederic Henry Hedge, wrote: "although it preserves the structural and lineal type of the face, and is not without a certain complacent beauty, [it] fails utterly with its milky mildness and placid vacuity to give us the Emerson we knew and revered. Compared with the London photograph by Elliott and Fry [see 1873], it seems almost imbecile. The master's sweetness is there, but the intellect—?"

Stephen Alonzo Schoff (1818–1904), a well-known American engraver, also engraved an image of Walt Whitman for the frontispiece to the 1860 edition of *Leaves of Grass*. He later made a larger version of the Emerson image for sale, some copies of which were struck on rice paper in a limited printing.

LATE 1850S

Emerson in the late 1850s

Three versions have been noted:

(A)

From a carte-de-visite published by Edward Anthony (1818–1888), 501 Broadway, New York. Anthony moved to this address on 1 May 1860.

Variants of this image are published in "Portraits," with the caption "From a photograph taken in Chicago in 1856," and in *W*, 7, described in the "List of Illustrations" as "From a daguerreotype taken in the West in 1859."

If the photograph was indeed taken during one of Emerson's western lecture trips, it could have been taken at the end of 1855 or early in 1856 or 1857 but not in 1859, when Emerson did not travel west. He did head west in January and February of 1860, which presents another possibility. Emerson failed to mention sitting for this portrait in his letters, journals, or account books. Whether it was truly taken on a western trip is unknown.

(B)

No further information is known.

(C)

Published in Amos Bronson Alcott, *Sonnets and Canzonets*, and Charles J. Woodbury, *Talks with Ralph Waldo Emerson*.

Note: For a discussion of the misattribution of image (A) to Mathew Brady, see Appendix A.

LATE 1850S

Emerson in the late 1850s

R. W Emerson.

A copy at JM has "Charles Taber & Co., Manufacturers, New-Bedford, Mass." on the back. Taber was a partner in a photographic manufactory business in 1862 and by 1871 was its sole owner. No further information is known.

1858

William James Stillman, The Philosophers' Camp in the Adirondacks *(1858)*

William James Stillman's *The Philosophers' Camp in the Adirondacks* depicts a visit by the Adirondack Club—an offshoot of the Saturday Club—to the Adirondack wilderness in 1858. The trip was organized by Stillman (1828–1901), a talented man of wide-ranging interests and occupations, who was a friend of a number of Saturday Club members. He trained as an artist with Frederic Church—American landscape painter of the Hudson River School—and in London, where he was influenced by the pre-Raphaelites. In 1855, he founded *The Crayon: A Journal Devoted to the Graphic Arts and the Literature Related to Them*, and through this periodical became acquainted with a number of the thinkers and writers of his time.

An outdoorsman, Stillman persuaded James Russell Lowell and some of his friends in the Saturday Club to make a camping expedition to Follansbee Pond in the Adirondacks in August

Enlarged image of Emerson

1858. The party included Emerson, Lowell, Louis Agassiz, Estes Howe, Jeffries Wyman, John Holmes, Ebenezer Rockwood Hoar, Horatio Woodman, Amos Binney, Stillman, and a number of local Adirondack guides. Others were invited but declined to go.

Emerson stands alone in the center, between two trees. Hoar is the first figure from Emerson to the viewer's right. Behind Emerson, at the left, a cluster of campers (a guide, Holmes, Howe, and Wyman) is grouped around scientific naturalist Agassiz, who is dissecting a fish. In front of Emerson, on the right side of the painting, marksmen (including Hoar, Lowell, and Woodman) engage in target practice under Stillman's direction (Stillman stands elbow-to-elbow with the figure raising a gun). For additional information on this outing, as well as Emerson's poetic version of it, see *CW*, 9:340–354.

In his *Autobiography of a Journalist*, Stillman acknowledged his response to Emerson as the most important of the campers:

> [T]his image of Emerson claiming kinship with the forest stands out alone, and I feel as if I had stood for a moment on a mount of transfiguration, and seen, as if in a vision, the typical American, the noblest in the idealization of . . . all the race. . . . [A]s a unique, idealized individuality, Emerson looms up in that Arcadian dream more and more the dominant personality. It is as character, and not as accomplishment or education, that he holds his own in all comparisons with his contemporaries, the fine, crystallized mind, the keen, clear-faceted thinker and seer.

Stillman's painting has been reproduced multiple times. It appeared as a photogravure plate in the 1904 edition of *Poems* issued by Houghton Mifflin as part of the Autograph Centenary Edition, and, recently, in Stephen L. Dyson, *The Last Amateur: The Life of William J. Stillman*, and James Schlett, *A Not Too Greatly Changed Eden: The Story of the Philosophers' Camp in the Adirondacks*.

The painting and a simplified version of Edward Emerson's key were included in *The Early Years of the Saturday Club*.

Note: Edward Waldo Emerson, key to Stillman's *The Philosopher's Camp in the Adirondacks* (below). Edward misdated the expedition as "1857."

1858

Emerson with Edith and Edward in 1858

This photograph—apparently a studio photograph—was published in *J, 9*, titled "A Virgil Lesson (Mr. Emerson, his younger daughter and son)." Described in the list of illustrations in that volume as a photogravure from an ambrotype taken in 1858, it shows Emerson at fifty-five seated with his seventeen-year-old younger daughter Edith and his son Edward (aged fourteen) standing to his right. The three are looking at an open book on Emerson's lap.

The photograph depicts father and children engaged in what Edward Emerson later described as a regular activity of the Emerson household. In *Emerson in Concord*, Edward wrote "He liked to read and recite to us poems or prose passages a little above our heads, and on Sunday mornings often brought into the dining-room something rather old for us." Whether or not the three were actually discussing Virgil in this photograph, reading the classics was part of family life for the Emerson children.

There appears to be no contemporary reference in Emerson's writings or those of family members to the taking of this photograph, so it may be that the date 1858 is approximate rather than exact. Regardless, the date works with the ages Edith and Edward appear to be in the image.

The British poet Arthur Hugh Clough expressed a desire for a copy of this in 1861. Ellen Emerson felt it was "the best that was ever taken" of her father.

1858[?]

Emerson in 1858[?]

Two versions have been noted:

(A)   (B)

Image (A) was used on a carte-de-visite issued by Silsbee, Case & Co. at 299½ Washington Street in Boston (the address on the verso in three of the four located copies). George M. Silsbee (1830–1900) and John G. Case (1818–1879) worked together at that address between 1858 and 1862.

Image (B) appears in *W*, 11, captioned in the "List of Illustrations" as "From an ambrotype taken in the West in 1858." Emerson made no western lecture tour in 1858, but he did travel west early in 1857.

Emerson may have had a photograph taken in Chicago or Cincinnati, but no documentation to support that possibility has turned up. Despite Sanborn and *W*, version (A) of the portrait clearly represents the original version; and certainly the date span of the partnership of Silsbee and Case matches the approximate date the photograph was taken.

1859

Bust of Emerson in 1859 by Sidney H. Morse

Three views have been noted:

(A)

From 1865 to 1872, the Reverend Sidney H. Morse (1833–1903) was editor of the monthly liberal Unitarian magazine *The Radical*. However, early in his life he "entered the marble business with an uncle, and it was there that his artistic tendencies got their first encouragement. He learned to cut and carve in marble." After *The Radical* expired, he returned to sculpting. According to George Willis Cooke, Morse "gained some distinction as a sculptor with his busts of Channing, Emerson, Lincoln, Whitman, and others."

(B)   (C)

There were two separate busts of Emerson by Morse, a small one done from life, and a large one completed after Emerson's death. Sanborn believed "Morse's reduced bust, at Concord, is unlucky in pose and expression; the full bust is better, as I remember it." The CFPL Photofile includes a 1982 photograph of the small bust (image [A]), then in the possession of David Emerson. Image (B) was reproduced in *W*, 4, captioned "Ralph Waldo Emerson in 1859" (the "List of Illustrations" has "From a bust by Sidney M. Morse in 1859"), and image (C) was reproduced as the frontispiece to the Standard Library Edition of *Essays: First Series* similarly identified. Since there is no reference to Morse's bust in Emerson's letters or journals or in family papers, this date is unconfirmed and may actually be later.

Morse recalled Emerson's sitting for him: "Emerson's features were firm and flashing, and o'er cast with the light of a never absent pleasing or happy expectation; but they verged nigh to caricature. A man must have a great thinking going on in the grey tissues of him, a bold and buoyant spirit, to carry them majestically as he did," and concerning "the difference in the expression of the two sides of the face" in the small bust, it was "in the original. His face was not, seen in front, in balance or proportion, one side with the other." He also wrote to Edward Emerson that Waldo "seemed to think it a difficult task for any artist" to capture his image, "saying to me once in my studio . . . 'When I look in the glass, I do not see myself. Can you see more or better than I.'"

Copies of Morse's bust of Emerson were advertised for sale in the August-September 1891 *Poet-Lore* for $7.50. Morse began "a new series of life-size" busts in 1894, including one of Emerson "after the smaller one . . . which has met with the warm approval of Mr. Edward Emerson," which sold for $12.50.

Note: See Appendix A for information about a large bust of Emerson done by Morse after the former's death.

BETWEEN 1860 AND 1868

Emerson between 1860 and 1868 by James Wallace Black

Five versions have been noted:

(A)   (B)

The Boston photographer James Wallace Black took a cluster of photographs of Emerson between 1860 and 1868 in two or more sittings. (Emerson's garb in the Black portraits suggests at least two sittings.)

Showing Emerson dressed in a tailcoat, image (A) depicts the subject standing as if to lecture. Behind him is a tied-back curtain that appears as a distinctive prop in most of the Black images of Emerson. The peculiarly sloping shoulders observed by writers on Emerson's appearance stand out in this pose.

Sanborn described this image as "a good likeness of the man as he stood at the beginning of his lecture, before gesture and facial expression began to give fuller effect to his grave and melodious voice." The image reflects the demeanor of the subject preparing to lecture as described by an audience member in Manchester, England: "He came on the platform in . . . [a] simple, quiet, almost careless and indifferent manner."

The copy at HNE of image (A) is captioned on the reverse: "BLACK   PHOTO. 173 Washington St., Boston." Black worked out of 173 Washington Street between 1860 and 1874. The JM copy of image (A) gives Black's address at 333 Washington Street, where he worked between 1875 and 1901. As with so many Emerson photographs, the image has been variously dated in publications: a plate of it in *W* placed it at 1857, and Sanborn dated it at 1869.

In the photograph of Emerson in the lecture stance (A) he wears a tailcoat, which supports the possibility that image (B), where he wears a frockcoat, and the other portraits (where his style of coat cannot be determined with certainty) resulted from multiple sittings.

The only located copy of image (B) is blank on the reverse. The attribution of it to Black is based primarily on the tell-tale curtain that appears in it and in Black images of Emerson positively identifiable through printed captions on the verso. Because this carte-de-visite bears no dateable photographer's address on the verso, its potential date span might actually be more inclusive than between 1860 and 1868. However, Emerson here appears roughly the same age as in other more dateable Black images (a dangerous criterion for dating portrait photographs, but perhaps not so unreliable when a date span rather than a specific date is under discussion).

(C1)

(C2)

Joel Myerson and Leslie Perrin Wilson 47

(c3)   (d)

Unlike the Black photograph of Emerson in the lecture stance (A), the standing Emerson here shown depicts the subject in an almost jaunty pose, with his right knee slightly bent (B). Black relied on the book in Emerson's hand rather than on his demeanor to suggest his status as a man of letters. This may be the picture that Ellen calls "the next best" picture of Emerson, after "The Virgil Lesson," one "which has never been copied, a large photograph in an overcoat which makes him appear a very portly person." However, given the fact that only one copy of this image has been located, it may not have been one that Emerson especially liked and that he consequently declined to have copied when he needed photographs for publicity or personal purposes.

The tied-back curtain appears in two other Black photographs shown here, (c1) and (E), in both of which Emerson is seated. (He sits in two different chairs in these photographs.) On the verso of two cartes-de-visite of image (c1) in which Emerson holds a book in his left hand and rests his left elbow on a table is printed "J. E. TILTON & CO. . . . | 161 *Wash*^{n}. *St.* | BOSTON. | PHOTOGRAPHED BY BLACK." Photograph publisher John E. Tilton & Company was located at 161 Washington Street between 1859 and 1872, which supports the date span for this cluster of images by Black.

The head-and-shoulders images (c2) and (c3) are clearly derived from image (c1).

Image (D) is a variation of image (C1) and the only located copy has the same publication information on the back (Tilton and Black) as do two cartes-de-visite of image (C1). Here, while Emerson holds a book in his left hand, he rests his right elbow on a table covered with a cloth identical to that in (C1).

In image (E), Emerson's hands are clasped in his lap. Sanborn identified it as "a photograph by Black" and reproduced it. It is reproduced in the June 1903 *Bookman* as "From a photograph in the Alexander Ireland Collection, kindly supplied by Mr. Charles W. Sutton, Free Reference Library, King Street, Manchester. *Photo by J. W. Black, Boston*." The back of one copy of this card has the same information as in image (C1) except the credit line to Black is omitted, while another copy has "J. W. Black, 173 Washington Street" on the back.

(E)

Note: The image at left, published by J. Gurney & Son, 707 Broadway, New York, may be from the Black sittings.

Jeremiah Gurney (1812–1886) began as a daguerreotypist in the early 1840s and joined in a partnership with son Benjamin Gurney (1833–1899) in 1860. They were at 707 Broadway between 1858 and 1869.

Joel Myerson and Leslie Perrin Wilson 49

1861

Bust of Emerson in 1861 by Thomas Ridgeway Gould

Two versions have been noted:

(A)   (B)

Version (A) is in marble (20½" high); version (B) is in plaster (25" high).

Thomas Ridgeway Gould (1818–1881) began his working life in dry goods before taking up sculpture, first as an avocation, then as his profession. He studied with artist Seth Wells Cheney in the early 1850s. As a sculptor, Gould appealed to the tastes of his time and met with acclaim and financial success. He opened a studio in Boston and exhibited at the Athenæum. His dry goods business ruined by the Civil War, he went to Italy in 1868 and opened a studio in Florence, where he died in 1881.

Gould may have begun working on this bust in late 1859, for on 11 January 1860, Emerson wrote a friend that, due to his injured foot, he must decline the latter's "kind proposal in behalf of seeing the bust of Mr Gould." Gould, in a letter to Emerson of 27 February, states that Emerson visited his studio on 16 January.

Lidian Emerson wrote her daughter Edith on 11 May 1861 that she and Waldo had "made an appointment" with Gould and would "go and see a bust he has made of father—mostly from recollection. He had only two sittings. Next day we went, with Ellen and Aunt Susan [Bridge Jackson] & Uncle Charles [Jackson]—to Mr Gould's studio—and found that the bust was really excellent. We all like it. I am glad that there is at last something that does not caricature your poor Papa. This bust will refute, to posterity, some of the slander going round, about him in the form of photographs &c.—not excepting Rowse's last." Ellen

Emerson also considered it "pretty good." Lidian's enthusiasm notwithstanding, the finished piece presents a vacuous and unsatisfactory Emerson—Sanborn called it an "amateur bust"—especially as compared with Daniel Chester French's 1879 bust.

Emerson and Gould corresponded and paid visits to each other's homes. In a letter written in May 1863, Gould was sorry that Emerson and Edith called on him in Boston when he was not home and commented that they "saw the bust in a bad light," apparently referring to the bust of Emerson.

Gould's marble version of the bust was presented by the sculptor to Harvard in 1865. Concord's plaster version was presented to the town's new public library in the fiscal year 1873/74 by Bronson Alcott. Alcott had written Gould on 1 October 1873—the day the Concord Free Public Library was dedicated—to postpone for financial reasons the purchase of a bust, presumably the Emerson in plaster, mentioning in a postscript the possibility that he might see the sculptor at the dedication ceremonies later that day. A mounted photograph of Gould's bust of Emerson serves as the frontispiece to the 1865 edition of Alcott's *Emerson*, and Lidian Emerson thought that "the best likeness of Mr Emerson extant."

1863 OR 1864

Emerson in 1863 or 1864 by Case and Getchell

Boston photographers John G. Case and William H. Getchell (1829–1910) worked in partnership in 1863 and 1864 at 299½ Washington Street. This carte-de-visite showing a three-quarters Emerson, seated, with his right hand resting on a table, must have been taken during that period.

There has been some confusion over the identity of the photographer. One carte-de-visite version exists with the imprint of Silsbee, Case & Co. at 299½ Washington Street in Boston on the verso. George M. Silsbee and John G. Case worked together at that address between 1858 and 1862. Another carte-de-visite exists with the imprint of "J. W. Black, | Photographer, | 173 Washington St. Boston" printed on the verso. Sanborn was familiar with the Black version of the photograph and reproduced it in "Portraits," captioned as "by Black" (458). However, James Wallace Black partnered with Case from 1865 to 1868. Black apparently republished this image taken by his partner prior to their association. Certainly the portrait lacks the curtain and tie-back used as background in nearly all the other Emerson images attributed to Black. Moreover, an argument can be made that Emerson appears fuller in face and figure than he does in the cluster of images known to have been taken by Black.

This may be the image Emerson referred to in an 18 August 1863 entry in his account book: "Pd for photographs of self   1.50."

1864

Painting of Emerson in 1864 by William Henry Furness Jr.

Sanborn described this picture as "by a good but not a great artist," William Henry Furness Jr. (1828–1867), and erroneously dated it "about 1865." He also gave the background to the painting:

> The early sittings for this portrait were in my house on the Sudbury Road in Concord, then unoccupied by me, and convenient to Mr. Furness, who lived in the vicinity. As I saw it from week to week, while painting, it seemed to me a good likeness of Emerson in his quiet and domestic character,—not strong in effect, and the reverse of Scott's in color, but pleasing, and deserving to be engraved. It was copied and engraved many years after by Miss Sartain of Philadelphia, and then did not please so much,—the copyist having added or subtracted something, I thought, to mar the simplicity of the picture. But it preserves the expression of those few years following the Civil War, when none but Emerson himself noted the approach of old age, and when his step in country lane or forest path was still as firm, his serene soul as unclouded as of yore.

Emily Sartain (1841–1927) was, like her father John Sartain (1808–1897), an eminent engraver (see image in *Notes*).

Another resident of Concord at this time, the poet William Ellery Channing, wrote a friend on 16 September 1864, "Furness lives at the Pritchard's and has been all summer taking Mr E. & Edith. Mrs E. says it will add another to the dreadful looking people he sits for,—he always declares his pictures look like malefactors." The entire Emerson family responded to

Edith's image with enthusiasm when it was delivered in March 1866, and Waldo called it "an admirable picture" and "a perpetual ornament & memorial dearly prized."

William Henry Furness, the painter's father and Emerson's Boston Latin School classmate, first wrote on 15 December 1871 about printing "a dozen or two" of Sartain's engraving, saying that while "the few of your friends who have seen it here are entirely pleased with it," he nevertheless "shall not consider that I have an official imprimatur without the favourable opinion of your family circle." Emerson responded on the seventeenth:

> At home again, I found your letter, & your Sartain copy of William Furness's picture, safely arrived. I have, as I suppose all old people have, a little terror at facing one's own face,—nay, I think I have a good deal of unwillingness, increasing on each experiment. . . . Well, my alarm was not a little relieved on drawing out & positing the head. It was certainly a kinder & more desireable figure & expression than I fear any photograph would give me. My wife was called, & instantly adopted it, & declared it was not only a good picture, but an excellent likeness,—better than any other. My daughter Ellen found it good, & Elizabeth Hoar found in it a likeness of all the Emersons;—so that nothing is left me but to express my thanks to Miss Sartain, the artist, & to yourself for your steadfast tenderness to your friend, which led your son to this work, which it seems was so skilfully & masterly done. . . . So you shall do what you & Miss Sartain think proper with this drawing, with the goodwill of this household. If she prints copies, I shall be glad to have her send me, say, 12 copies at the fixed price.

Furness replied three days later that he would send twelve copies of the mezzotint engraving (see *Notes*) gratis.

After the artist died in the spring of 1867, his father wrote Emerson on 31 March, "I do not consider his portrait of you . . . as good as he would have made it—I advised him not to finish it, to keep it on hand indefinitely & work upon it as he might have opportunity."

1866

Bas-relief of Emerson in 1866 by Charles Akers

Charles Akers (1836–1906), a Maine-born portrait artist, was introduced in 1866 by James Russell Lowell to his distinguished friends so that Akers could model them in "life-size" bronze bas-reliefs in order to make his mark in the Boston artists' market. Akers arrived in Concord on 24 July 1866 for a week's stay.

Of Emerson, Akers later recalled

> Mr. Emerson, my next sitter, was the slowest of movement, and in appearance most leisurely. . . . Upon my arrival at Concord, I found him engaged in some outdoor affairs. . . . A great ugly straw hat made the only change I noticed in his apparel; but that was startling. I had always seen him in the same black, formal garments, rather antiquated in style, very neat and precise, and with that wonted air which made one feel that he never had worn or could wear anything else. His tall, spare figure, narrow, sloping shoulders and this peculiar mode of dress made him conspicuous in any association. His face was equally striking . . . . It did not directly reveal his great intellectuality, but rather seemed stamped with an air of extreme refinement and fastidiousness, with something of the expression we notice in the more youthful bust of Cicero. The forehead was neither high nor broad, the whole face narrow and aquiline, the head rising very much toward the back.

1868

Emerson in 1868 by John Notman and Frank Rowell

First sitting
Three versions have been noted:

(A) (B)

These three sometimes misdated photographs were clearly the products of a single sitting. According to the printed caption on the bottom of a cabinet card version of the photograph, they are the work of "John Sloan Notman, with Frank Rowell, Studio, 25 Winter Street, Boston."

John Sloan Notman (1830–1879) was a younger brother of successful Montreal photographer William Notman (1826–1891), who emigrated from Scotland in the mid-1850s. Having worked for William in Canada, John established a photographic business on Tremont Street in Boston late in 1866. His brother William and brother-in-law J. M. Gatehouse were associated with the Boston business, as was photographer Frank Rowell (1832–1900). John Notman moved his operation to 25 Winter Street in 1868, then shut it down that same year and returned to Canada. Even though he remained in Boston for only two years, Notman's portrait work was noticed and praised in print as artistic and fashionable. Certainly the Notman images of Emerson display a staging and use of props calculated to suggest personality and status elegantly.

Emerson, his family, and his correspondents were silent on the circumstances of his sitting for Notman. Nevertheless, the fact that Notman worked from 25 Winter Street only in 1868 establishes a reasonably firm date for the images. The collaboration of Notman and Rowell in 1868 has elsewhere been observed. However, these Emerson images have been dated variously (at 1855, for example, in the July/August 1987 *American Heritage* and at 1865 in the manuscript identification on the verso of an Allen & Rowell copy of image [B]).

Photographers Allen & Rowell of Boston, who worked out of Notman's former 25 Winter Street address between 1874 and 1892, issued a later cabinet card version of at least one of the three Emerson images. Sanborn reproduced image (C) as by "Allen and Rowell."

(c)

Emerson noted in his account book for 29 April 1868 "Pd Notman for 12 photographs of Ellen 5.00" and on 16 May 1868 "Pd Notman for 12 photographs of Mrs L. E. 5." While the account books do not mention a picture of Emerson, he did write on 25 December 1868 to a friend who had requested a picture of him, "I do not find at home a single card of Notman's sitting figure," strongly suggesting that Waldo, as well as Ellen and Lidian, sat for Notman at approximately the same time.

Second sitting
Three versions have been noted:

(D)

(E)

(F)

Differences in the furniture indicate that images (D)–(F) are from a different sitting (possibly sittings) than are images (A)–(C).

Roger Hall reproduces and dates image (D) as 1868. The desk is identical to ones in pictures taken of "an unidentified gentleman" and Charles Cleveland, both in 1868.

The cabinet card of image (E) has "Published by A. A. Childs & Co., 127 Tremont Street, Boston" at the bottom front. Childs was active at that address between 1868 and 1874, and, again, between 1889 and 1891.

1868[?]

Emerson in 1868[?] by Augustus Marshall

Augustus Marshall (ca. 1835–1916) was practicing at the Studio Building (106 Tremont Street) between 1863 and 1867, and then at 145 Tremont Street between 1867 and 1882.

1868

Emerson with his grandson Ralph Emerson Forbes in 1868

Four versions have been noted:

(A)

Ralph Emerson Forbes, the son of Edith and William Hathaway Forbes, was born on 10 July 1866. John Murray Forbes was Emerson's daughter Edith's father-in-law.

Both located copies of image (A) and the copy of image (C) identify the photographer as John A. Whipple, 297 Washington Street, an address he moved to in 1865.

Image (B) was reproduced and dated 1868 in *LetETE*. Image (C) is inscribed on the back "W[illiam]. H[athaway]. Forbes" and dated 1868.

Either image (D1) or (D2) may be the "photographic head" Emerson sent to friends in 1867 or 1869.

Sanborn described image (D1) as "From a photograph by Marshall," and *W*, 8, called it "From a photograph taken in a group in 1868."

Image (D2) was published in the June 1903 London *Bookman* as "From a photograph in the Alexander Ireland Collection, kindly supplied by Mr. Charles W. Sutton, Free Reference Library, King Street, Manchester. *Photo by Allen and Rowell, Boston*."

Emerson with Ralph Emerson Forbes and John Murray Forbes

(B)

(C)

(D1)

(D2)

1871

Emerson in 1871 by William Shew

The front of the only located copy of this carte-de-visite has an embossed "Wm. Shew" and the back, while partially torn when removed from a pasted mount, shows that it was produced by William Shew's Photographic Establishment, 145 Kearney Street, San Francisco. Shew (1820–1903) established his gallery in San Francisco in 1851.

Emerson traveled to California in April-May 1871, staying in San Francisco from 21 April through 2 May and, again, during 15–19 May. On 18 May, according to James Bradley Thayer, who accompanied Emerson (just shy of his sixty-eighth birthday) on the trip, he sat "at the request of some friends, for his photograph." That this image is probably the one made for "some friends" is reflected in its scarcity: only one copy has been located and it has not been reproduced.

1873

Emerson in 1873 in London by Elliott and Fry

Five versions have been noted:

(A1)

(A2)

Joseph John Elliott (1835–1903) and Clarence Edmund Fry (1840–1897) began their collaboration in 1863 at 55 Baker Street, London. In 1885 they expanded to 55 and 56 Baker Street and in 1886 to 7 Gloucester Terrace. In the 1890s, their work was distributed in New York City by Frank Hegger's Photographic Depot. The various locations help date the images in this entry.

On 24 July 1872 a fire partially destroyed Emerson's house in Concord. While the house was being restored, Emerson and his daughter Ellen traveled abroad, stopping twice in London, from 6–13 November 1872 and from 5–27 April 1873. These pictures were taken during the latter stay, when more time was available for a sitting. A copy of image (A1) in

THE LATE RALPH WALDO EMERSON.
ELLIOTT & FRY. Copyright 55&56. BAKER ST. LONDON. W.

(B)

ELLIOTT & FRY   Copyright   55, BAKER ST.
PORTMAN SQ.

(C)

ELLIOTT & FRY   Copyright   55, BAKER ST.
PORTMAN SQ.

(D)

RALPH WALDO EMERSON.
ELLIOTT & FRY   Copyright   55, BAKER S?

(E1)

ELLIOTT & FRY   Copyright   55, BAKER S?
PORTMAN SQ?

(E2)

the Carlyle House, London, is inscribed by Thomas Carlyle "R. W. Emerson (May 1873)." Image (A2) is clearly derived from image (A1), just as image (E2) is derived from image (E1). Also, Emerson was in better physical shape in April than in November, making that a more likely time for the sitting, for as Ellen commented about her father in a letter home from London on 16–18 April 1873, "Everyone says here that he looks another man from what he was in November." There are no references in Emerson's letters or journals to this sitting, but Ellen wrote her sister Edith on 20 May 1873 that she had picked up a picture of her father while in London.

The National Portrait Gallery, London, has a copy negative of image (B) made by Elliott & Fry of their own exhibition print of Emerson.

Image (C) is known only through its reprinting in Kenneth Walter Cameron, *Ralph Waldo Emerson's Reading*, which provides no information about the source of the image.

1873

Emerson in 1873 by Eliphalet J. Foss

Five versions have been noted:

(A)

(B)

(C)

(D)

Ralph Waldo Emerson.

(E)

Foss's head-and-shoulders photograph of Emerson at seventy was taken just after the subject's return from his third and final trip abroad, following the July 1872 fire that severely damaged his home on the Cambridge Turnpike. The portrait shows an alert and poised Emerson with his signature small smile.

Eliphalet J. Foss (1840–1923) maintained a photographic studio at 13 Tremont Row in Boston starting in 1867; in 1872, he moved to 171½ Tremont Street, where he remained until 1874. He later operated a studio in Malden, Massachusetts. Foss was a patent-holder for several photographic improvements.

Emerson left no comment about sitting for the photographer or about his reaction to the image, though he did make two undated cryptic entries in his pocket diary for 1874: "My Foss Photograph from W. Hunt for godchild & Mrs [Corinne] Chamberlaine" and "~~Photographs at Foss's~~."

Sanborn wrote of this photograph:

> His return was in May, 1873; and about that time must be dated the photograph engraved for the posthumous edition of his poems, in 1884—the best of the later portraits. It was taken by a Boston photographer named Foss; but the negative got broken, and in that state passed into the hands of H. G. Smith, of the Studio Building, Boston, who repaired the damage and has since printed many copies from it. Dr. Emerson says: "There is no good picture of my father in his old age except this, of which there is a drawing [i.e., engraving] in the Riverside Poems." It was made, Miss [Ellen] Emerson tells me, soon after she returned with her father from Europe, in June, 1873, and exhibits him as he looked with the refreshment of that last visit to his friends in England and Paris and the wonders of Egypt. The Scott picture, then, for the serious reformer's attitude, and the Boston photograph for the serene old sage of threescore and ten.

Edith Forbes wrote her sister Ellen on 23 May 1873, "When the first photographs came we had great rejoicing over Father's to see him look so well—and to have caught the lovely sweetness that everyone says has been growing in his face in the last two years or so . . . . [¶] . . . Next came the second photographs. I did not like them so well."

Horatio G. Smith, who issued the later cabinet card from Foss's negative, ran a photographic business in Boston at various locations between 1862 and 1909. He was located in the Studio Building from 1867 to 1905.

Image (A) appears over a printed inscription by Emerson as the frontispiece (the image itself is a pasted-on photograph) to Ireland's *Ralph Waldo Emerson* and is said to have been "taken about 1873." A cabinet card has been noted with this information written on the back: "given to me by Wendell Phillips winter of 1873–74, taken lately." Foss's image was used for the frontispiece in the 1884 Riverside Edition of Emerson's *Poems*, engraved by J. A. J. Wilcox, Boston, from an undetermined image, and image (B) was later published in *W*, 10: frontispiece, where it is dated 1873. A cabinet card of image (C) by Charles Pollock (1828–1900) of Boston could have been made at any time between 1888 and 1892. A cabinet card of image (D) was published by the studios of William Notman, Montreal, Toronto, and Halifax.

1873 OR 1874

Bust of Emerson in 1873 or 1874 by Martin Milmore

MILMORE'S BUST OF EMERSON. (*Owned by T. G. Appleton.*)

Only known through this drawing by Robert Lewis in [George B. Bartlett], "Ralph Waldo Emerson," in Arthur Gilman et al., *Poets' Homes*.

Martin Milmore (1844–1883) was an Irish-born Boston sculptor who achieved a considerable contemporary reputation for his public statuary (much of it undertaken in conjunction with his brother Joseph) and for busts of well-known men. He went to Italy in the 1870s and later returned to Boston, where he died.

Emerson had praised Milmore's statues in Horticultural Hall in 1866 as "surprisingly good at first & second sight." On 12 November 1871, he wrote sculptor and poet Anne Whitney, who apparently had asked him to sit for a bust, "I have no time to sit for months to come. . . . Mr [Wendell] Phillips pressed me many months ago, urging the wishes of Mr Milmore . . . to sit to him. At last I promised to go & see Mr M., & see some of his works. I went once & failed to find him: but I still hold myself bound to visit him, & should find it embarrassing to refuse him, except on the ground that I would not sit at all to a sculptor. For I have heard of his desire for years."

It is not clear if or when Emerson sat for Milmore. However, documentation shows that Milmore did, in fact, sculpt a bust of Emerson. Ellen Emerson wrote her sister Edith on 14 February 1872 that Waldo "went to the sculptor Milmore's room. Mr M. wants to have him sit for a bust, and begged hard and Father showed him the impregnable surface of wily diplomacy, but still 'he sat & begged.'" A footnote to Emerson's letter to Anne Whitney in *L* described an 8 September 1872 letter from Phillips as "asking an opportunity for Milmore to finish his bust of Emerson before the sculptor should leave for Rome." The note also cited an undated fragment of Emily Mervine Drury's diary in which appears the comment, "Mr Wendell Phillips says that Ralph Waldo Emerson's head is a very difficult one to render in marble but that Milmore's bust of him is serene."

Milmore's obituary in the *New York Times* stated that several of his busts, including that of Emerson, were "greatly esteemed." Indeed, the 1874 catalogue for the *Twelfth Exhibition of the Massachusetts Charitable Mechanic Association* shows that Milmore's marble bust of Emerson—owned by Thomas Gold Appleton—took a silver medal at that event. However, three years later the Philadelphia *Times* announced "Mr. Martin Milmore has been commissioned to make a bust of Emerson for Mr. T. G. Appleton, of Boston," possibly a copy. Daniel Chester French, who produced his own bust of Emerson in 1879, carved a plaster cast relief titled "The Angel of Death Staying the Hand of the Sculptor" as a memorial to Milmore and his brother, and it won a medal at the Paris Salon of 1892; his bronze relief of it marks Milmore's grave in Boston.

MID-1870S

Emerson in the mid-1870s by George Kendall Warren

Three versions have been noted:

(A1)   (A2)

A cabinet card with image (A2) has "Warren's Portraits, 465 Washington Street" printed on the back. George Kendall Warren (1824–1884), a prominent Boston photographer, worked at that address between 1875 and 1882.

A cabinet card with image (A3), identified on the front as from Bruckmann's Collection, Geo. Kirchner & Co., New York, is part of a series of altered cabinet cards originally published in Germany by Friedrich Bruckmann's Verlag, some of which were distributed by Kirchner. An 1883 advertisement for J. F. Schipper & Co. announced the cabinet card of Emerson as "Just added."

Image (B) is known only through its printing in Kenneth Walter Cameron, *Ralph Waldo Emerson's Reading*, without information about the source of the image.

(A3)

(B)

(C)

Joel Myerson and Leslie Perrin Wilson 71

1875

Emerson, Samuel Bradford, and William Henry Furness in 1875
by Frederick Gutekunst

Four versions have been noted:

(A1)

(A2)

(B1)

(B2)

Joel Myerson and Leslie Perrin Wilson 73

(C)

(D)

Emerson—then approaching seventy-two—sat for four portraits at the Philadelphia studio of Frederick Gutekunst in March 1875. The three group portraits show Emerson seated around a table with his Boston Latin School friends Samuel Bradford and William Henry Furness (two showing Emerson on the left, Bradford in the middle, and Furness on the right; one showing Bradford on the left, Emerson in the middle, and Furness on the right).

Frederick Gutekunst (1831–1917) became a commercial photographer in the 1850s and was Philadelphia's premier portrait photographer from the 1860s through the remainder of the century. He took many photographs of Civil War soldiers and leaders. From 1866, his business was located at 712 Arch Street.

The images are rare among photographic portraits of Emerson in that they can be dated with some precision. Ellen Emerson, who was with her father in Philadelphia, wrote home to her mother on 20 March 1875: "Father shows unusual pleasure in the society of Mr. Furness and Mr. Bradford, and went with enthusiasm to be photographed with them."

Furness wrote from Philadelphia on 25 March 1875 to Emerson, who was then back in Concord:

> [Y]ou will surely not find it in your heart to condemn our photographic friend, Gutekunst, for taking advantage of the opportunity, &, when the pleasure of mankind was concerned, disregarding all considerations of personal veracity, &, at one of the sittings of the Three Boys, directing the attention of the sun particularly to yourself.

> I send you a specimen of the result. He says he honestly meant to take us all three, but Sam's & mine were failures, while yours was so good, he cut it out, & you have it with the others which I sent by this mail. Either the photographer aimed particularly at you, or the divinity you wot of, which is always whittling ends, got command of the instrument.

> We are all so pleased with this single head that, had I been an accomplice in its production, I should not be ashamed of it. After all Mr. G. puts the negative entirely at your disposal. If you say the word, it shall be destroyed.

> The other specimens which I send you are numbered 1, 2, 3 (the 4th was poor). Please let us know which is liked best, & of which you prefer to have a number. The photographer tells me they can be enlarged.

Two of the group portraits ([A1] and [C]) were used in *Records of a Lifelong Friendship*, and (A2) appeared as the frontispiece. Image (B1) was first reproduced in "Portraits."

On the twenty-ninth Ellen wrote to her cousin John Haven Emerson that the "photograph of 'The Three Boys' as Father and Mr Furness call it has come, indeed there are three different ones." Waldo wrote Furness on 3 April: "The photographs came, & I tried to compare & decide which to keep & which to burn, but was too glad to leave them to Ellen for judgment. Each was best to one sitter but Ellen shall choose."

Joel Myerson and Leslie Perrin Wilson 75

Horace Howard Furness (1833–1912), William Henry's son, commented upon this sitting:

> It was taken in more than one pose; one of these has been published, I believe [image (B1)]. But the first pose, which was discarded, is to me, in one regard, far and away the best, in that it is eminently characteristic both of Mr. Emerson, and of my father, who was, at the photographic instant, so lost in gazing with admiration at his friend, that he utterly forgot himself and, in resting his face in his hand, quite hid his own features [image (A)]. This gaze Mr. Emerson returned and unconsciously responded to it; his 'face is as a book wherein one may read' his lifelong love for my father from childhood onwards. In no other portrait of Mr. Emerson that I have ever seen has his benignant and exquisitely sweet and characteristic smile been so happily caught. My father had a photographic enlargement made of the head alone of Mr. Emerson [possibly image (A2)]. It hung until his death in his study, and he never varied the assertion that it is the best ever taken; in it he could distinctly and vividly trace the features and the expression of the little boy in petticoats, with whom he played with wooden blocks on the floor of his mother's room.

He continued, "Twice the position of the three sitters was changed by the photographer. But with what disastrous results! Three respectable, elderly gentlemen more self-conscious it would be hard to match!"

Sanborn wrote of the head-and-shoulders Gutekunst image of Emerson solo (image [A2]), "The Emerson has lately been enlarged by Gutekunst." Sanborn was apparently unaware that four group portraits were taken in Philadelphia, that one—deemed substandard by the photographer—was not used to print cabinet cards showing the three men together, and that the head-and-shoulders Emerson photograph was actually an enlargement from the figure of Emerson in the rejected image. Comparison of Emerson's head-and-shoulders images with the three surviving group photographs makes clear that image (A2) is from image (A1) and image (B2) is from image (B1), and image (D) must have come from the fourth (rejected) group portrait. The back of a cabinet card of image (B2) has written in hand: "Ralph Waldo Emerson. From a negative for which he sat May 11 [*sic*], 1875. From my friend F. Gutekunst."

1876

Edward Waldo Emerson and Emerson holding Charles Lowell Emerson in 1876

Two versions have been noted:

(A)

(B)

Charles Lowell Emerson (b. 3 July 1876) was the son of Emerson's son Edward and Annie Shepard Keyes, who were married in 1874. Image (A) was published in *LetETE* between letters of 23 January and 1 February 1877 describing visits to Bush by Edward, his wife, and their son.

These two pictures may be what Emerson referred to in his account book entry for 28 April 1877: "Paid Whipple, Metcalf & Welldon for Dagguer[e]otypes &c   17.00."

LATE 1870S

Emerson in the late 1870s by George Kendall Warren

Two versions have been noted:

(A)   (B)

Both located copies have "Warren's" on the front and "Warren's Portraits, 465 Washington Street, Boston" on the back. Warren was active at that address between 1875 and 1882.

These may be the pictures of which Ellen sent proofs to her sister Edith in February 1879.

1878

Sketch of Emerson in July 1878 by Wyatt Eaton

(Charles) Wyatt Eaton (1849–1896) studied in Paris between 1872 and 1876, where he worked under Jean-Leon Gérôme. Upon his return to America, he opened a studio in New York.

Eaton, to whom "it had been one of my most cherished desires to make a portrait of Emerson," was asked by the *Century Magazine* to make a series of portraits for engravings

Joel Myerson and Leslie Perrin Wilson 79

in it. While sitting, Emerson said, "'You must get through with this work as quickly as possible, for I am very old; I have but a little longer to live, and so much to do.' He explained that it was not new work he wished to do, but to arrange the work of his past years." About Emerson's mental state, Eaton commented, "The only faculty I could see that Emerson had lost was the memory of names and words. His mind upon all other subjects seemed to be perfectly clear." Ellen Emerson wrote her brother Edward that her father had met Eaton while in England in 1872–1873.

In July 1878, Sanborn "used to sit with Emerson in his study, to hold him in conversation while Mr. Wyatt Eaton was sketching the (unsuccessful) portrait reproduced with this paper." The result of

> these pleasant sittings in Emerson's study,—pleasant to the artist and to me, and not so apparently disagreeable to the sitter as such things often were,— was a disappointment when engraved; having far more the look of desolate, solitary age than was the usual aspect of Emerson in the summer of 1878. The mobility and liveliness of his face seemed to be left out, and a certain grimness called up from the inner consciousness of a man who knows that each year brings him nearer to the grave, escorted by the ills that wait on age. It could not be mistaken for the head of another man, and it was true to the framework of the sage's features and the vivacity of his eyes. But the ineffable sweetness was not there,—or but a lingering ray of it; and the hard, modern style of treating the engraving [by Cole; see *Note one*] . . . increased the dislike which most of us felt for the drawing. As a study, however, for a complete portrait of Emerson the moralist, it has real merit; nothing is there which might not have been in the original, and the underlying severity of this modified Puritan is plainly to be seen.

Sanborn described Emerson's reaction to the original portrait thus: "'I will show you what this man looks like'; and, proceeding from the dining-room, where we were sitting, to the study, he brought back his volume of Herrick, containing the profile of that robust poet, with his enormous Roman nose,—to which he pointed as his own *vera effigies*" (see *Note two*).

1879

Emerson in his study in 1879 by Augustus H. Folsom

First published in *CEC*, facing 53, and in color in *Exhibition*, 79. Augustus H. Folsom (d. 1926) opened his studio in Roxbury, Massachusetts, in 1879. He had prepared a series of interior and exterior images of CFPL soon after it opened in 1873.

Emerson and his relations seem to have been regular clients of Folsom: in 1889 he took a picture of the house Waldo's son-in-law William Hathaway Forbes built on Naushon Island, which Forbes's father, John Murray Forbes, had purchased in 1843.

1879

Bust of Emerson in 1879 by Daniel Chester French

Plaster bust

(A)

Marble bust

Two versions have been noted:

(B)   (C)

Sculptor Daniel Chester French (1850–1931) created the original clay model of his bust of Emerson from life in 1879, three years before his subject's death.

In 1876, French returned to America from Italy. While abroad, his Minute Man statue at the reconstructed North Bridge in Concord—the work that established him as a public artist—was dedicated. He set up a studio in Washington, resettled in 1878 in Concord, and in 1879 completed a studio next to his family's home on Sudbury Road.

French's bust of Emerson was created early in the sculptor's career. Because Emerson was a friend of the French family and a relative by marriage, there was a personal connection between artist and subject. French began work on the bust in March 1879. He went daily to Bush, where Emerson sat for him, and completed the original clay model in April. Plaster casts were made from the master mold that came from the clay model. One of the first plaster copies was presented to Emerson on 26 July 1879. Another copy (now at CFPL) was presented to the French family of Concord. Also in 1879, French began selling plaster casts of the bust for $30.00.

Emerson is famously reported to have commented on seeing the finished bust, "Dan, that's the face I shave." Ellen Emerson wrote John Haven Emerson and his wife Susie on 11–12 June, "I wonder whether you have heard that Dan French has made a bust of Father. It is good. I have no fault to find with it. We all consider it a piece of great good fortune. I am not sure that Edward is satisfied but Edith & I are and Mr [James Elliot] Cabot said 'I never expected to see anything so satisfactory.'"

French had to work hard to capture a vigorous, reactive Emerson. In his biography of Emerson, James Elliot Cabot reported French's comments on how difficult it had been to see beyond the frailty of the fading elder Emerson and to communicate the essence of what the man had been. French referred to Emerson's "almost child-like mobility that admitted of an infinite variety of expression, and made possible that wonderful 'lighting-up' of the face, so often spoken of by those who knew him," and lamented, "It was the attempt to catch that glorifying expression that made me despair of my bust. At the time I made it, as you know, Mr. Emerson had failed somewhat, and it was only now and then that I could see, even for an instant, the expression I sought."

Within a few years, French had a marble version of the bust carved in Italy. The first marble carving was given to Harvard in 1883 by the Higginson family. In 1884, a second marble carving (slightly different from the first) was presented to CFPL as "a gift from one hundred and thirty-five contributors, including Mr. French himself, who was the largest contributor."

Much later, in modelling his posthumous marble statue of Emerson seated (unveiled at CFPL in 1914), French drew upon his 1879 bust from life as well as on photographs of Emerson.

1879

Emerson and his extended family in 1879

Two sittings have been noted:

(A)

This portrait of the Emerson family grouped at the east door of their home on the Cambridge Turnpike in Concord is mounted in the Emerson family photograph album compiled in 1903 for the centennial of the birth of Ralph Waldo Emerson (now at CFPL). The typed caption pasted beneath it in the album reads "R. W. E. and L. J. E. and their descendents (1882?)." However, the year "1879" is clearly written by hand on the foundation of the house beneath the window to the left of the photograph.

    Edith W. Gregg identifies the photograph as taken at Thanksgiving Day 1879, which would have been 27 November. Her caption identifies the members of the group: "Standing, from left, Edward W. Emerson, Edward W. Forbes, Ellen T. Emerson, little Edith Forbes, RWE behind Cameron Forbes and Lidian Emerson behind Don Forbes, Edith E. Forbes holding little Waldo, and Ralph E. Forbes, far right. Seated is Annie Keyes Emerson with Charles." Since Emerson's baby grandson Waldo was born 28 February 1879, the

Thanksgiving dating of the photograph appears accurate. Rusk identifies the photographer as Augustus H. Folsom.

Ellen Emerson wrote to Gisela von Arnim Grimm on 22 January 1880 that "two days after Thanksgiving, (Thanksgiving is the New England family-festival) when we were all together, (All but my sister's husband [William Hathaway Forbes] who alas! had to go away on business)" a man "photographed the whole family, root & branch, on the East doorstep. . . . Father & Mother, seated; three children behind them in order of age, Edith with her baby. The little Edith behind her mother & looking over her grand-mother's shoulder. Edith's other four sons ranged on the edge of the step, on the left; and on the right, Edward's wife and his only child, his eldest son, and his third, are dead." This unlocated image must have been made at the same time as image (A).

Ellen Tucker Emerson and Emerson

Collection of the Massachusetts Historical Society.

(B)

This image of Emerson at seventy-six with his daughter Ellen was clearly taken at Thanksgiving 1879, when the Emerson and Forbes clans posed for a group photograph by the east door of Bush (image [A]). The clothing and overall appearance of both figures are identical in the two photographs, and both are posed by the door shutter against which they stood in the group photograph. Also, a bit of the long white gown worn by baby Waldo in the group image is visible at the right of the photograph.

EARLY 1880S

Emerson in the early 1880s by George Kendall Warren

One of the located copies has "Warren's" on the front and "Warren's Portraits, 465 Washington Street, Boston" on the back. Warren was active at that address between 1875 and 1882.

EARLY 1880S

Emerson in the early 1880s

Three versions have been noted:

(A)

(B)

(c)

Emerson's clothing, the chair in which he sits, and the studio backdrop are the same in all three images, which are clearly the product of the same sitting. No further information is known.

Joel Myerson and Leslie Perrin Wilson 89

EARLY 1880S

Emerson in the early 1880s by George Kendall Warren

Both located copies have "Warren's Portraits, 465 Washington Street, Boston" on the back. Warren was active at that address between 1875 and 1882. Emerson died in 1882 at nearly seventy-nine, making this one of his last photographs.

APPENDIX A
APOCRYPHAL IMAGES OF EMERSON

This Appendix contains images described as being of Emerson for which conclusive evidence is lacking or which are definitely not of Emerson.

1837

Silhouette and watercolor by Thomas Edwards

Reproduced in *The American Heritage Auction of Americana* and described as 8″ x 5¾″.

    Edwards (1795–1869) was born in London and worked in Boston from the 1830s through the 1850s. Primarily a painter and sketch artist, he also created silhouettes, including ones of John James Audubon and his wife. While the image matches descriptions of Emerson lecturing with his left hand at his side, the picture itself does not look like Emerson and the signature is different from those in other silhouettes by Edwards.

1841[?]

Drawing in 1841[?] by "W. M. T."

This is described by the Berg in a note on the reverse as being "Removed from: Emerson, R. W. Essays, London, 1841. Copy 1." It is pasted on the back of coated paper with "William M. Tuke" on the front. Tuke (1822–1903) was a banker and businessman in Saffron Walden, England, whose son, William Favill Tuke (1863–1940), became chair of Barclay's bank.

The attribution of this crude image to Emerson is based entirely on its location in *Essays.*

1847

Engraving in 1847 by Henry Clark Pidgeon

On 2 September 1847, Mary Howitt, co-editor of *Howitt's Journal*, wrote Emerson, who was on his British lecture tour, about supplying her with biographical information and a picture for publication, an offer he declined. Elizabeth Hoar wrote Emerson on 23 February 1848, "I saw your picture in Howitt's Journal. It was worse than I feared," but Emerson, in writing his wife earlier, on 10 February, declared he had "never seen the Howitt or Peoples Journal you mention."

Henry Clark Pidgeon (1807–1880) was a British watercolorist.

This image is included because it appears in an unsigned article "From our Manchester Correspondent" on "Emerson's Lectures" in *Howitt's Journal*, suggesting that it may have been done from life (it does, especially with the sloping shoulders, look like him during this period). The article contains this physical description of Emerson as well: "In due time Emerson made his appearance, and took his stand under the glaring jet of gas, which leaves the lecturer's face completely in shadow. He is thin and spare in figure, which probably makes him appear taller than he really is; but he must be above the middle height. The features of his profile are prominent, and the caverns in which his eyes glow, are beautifully shaped. The form of his head is good; a pile of forehead, much covered with hair, rests on his long, thin face."

A version of this image appeared in the 10 January 1852 *Gleason's Pictorial* with this information: "We present our readers herewith a fine likeness of Ralph Waldo Emerson, the distinguished lecturer, now in this city. Mr. Emerson is too well known, both by his voice and pen, to require any elaborate introduction in this connection; suffice it to say that the picture is a very faithful one, and does the original ample justice in the likeness":

PORTRAIT OF RALPH WALDO EMERSON.

Another version appeared in 1853 as the frontispiece to Emerson's *Essays and Orations*:

R. W. EMERSON.

1857

Bas-relief in 1857 by Joseph Carew

Attributed to Carew and dated on the basis of "J. Carew SC, 1857" appearing on the edge. According to the entry for it in the William Reese catalogue, it "was quite possibly sculpted from life."

Joseph Carew (ca. 1820–1870) was a Boston sculptor and monument maker who frequently exhibited at the Boston Athenæum and executed commissions at Mount Auburn Cemetery. In 1857, he was located at 143 Harrison Avenue in Boston, a few blocks from the Common.

There are no references to Carew in Emerson's letters and journals. Carew may have made this idealistic classical image of Emerson from sketches done when seeing him in downtown Boston or lecturing, or he may have worked from a contemporary engraving.

1857

Oliver Wendell Holmes and Emerson[?] in the Boston Public Garden in 1857

First published in Caroline Ticknor, *Dr. Holmes's Boston*, with the caption "The Beacon Street Side of the Public Garden, in 1857, showing Dr. Holmes and Ralph Waldo Emerson in Conversation." Although the people in the picture are described as Emerson in the white hat and Holmes in the black, the image is too small to ascertain with certainty that this is correct.

LATE 1850S

Emerson in the late 1850s attributed to Mathew Brady

This is identified in Robert D. Richardson Jr.'s *Emerson: The Mind on Fire* as "Emerson at 56. Photo from a carte de visite, derived in turn from a photo made by Matthew [*sic*] Brady in 1859."

Richardson has introduced the possibility of this photograph having been taken by Mathew Brady, but that attribution is based on slim evidence. Richardson used his own copy of the carte-de-visite portrait in his book and based his caption on information provided in the Cedric L. Robinson catalogue from which he bought it. The catalogue entry reads, "(EMERSON, RALPH WALDO) (BRADY, MATHEW, PHOTOGRAPHER). Carte de Visite Portrait. Photographic Print 3.3" x 2.2" on gilt-ruled printed card 3.45" x 2.4" . . . On back: 'EA' monogram (Edward Anthony Co.) and faint printing of 'Brady's National Gallery...' imprint. Photograph taken 1859, printed ca. 1860s." The dealer was wrong about the faint printing on the verso of the image, however: digital enlargement and enhancement cannot recover the identification of the firm, but there is a carte-de-visite identifying (on the verso) E. Anthony of 501 Broadway as the publisher. Brady's name does not appear on Richardson's copy of this image.

Cedric L. Robinson had some reason to make a connection between Brady and Anthony. Edward Anthony and his brother Henry were innovative manufacturers and sellers of cameras and photographic supplies and also publishers of their own stereographic views. Edward Anthony started out in the photographic business as a daguerreotypist. In the early 1840s, in partnership with Jonas M. Edwards, he preceded Brady in creating an extensive gallery of photographs of distinguished men in politics and other fields. Anthony later reproduced "quantities of photographic copies of the Brady collection in the size called cartes-de-visite." However, because it cannot be assumed that any carte-de-visite bearing Anthony's name was by Brady or even from Brady's studios, in the absence of other documentation showing that Emerson ever sat for Brady, it is a stretch to attribute this portrait to Brady.

Frederick Hill Meserve purchased some 13,000 glass plate negatives by Brady in 1902 and later used them to make the prints illustrating his *Historical Portraits: A Collection of Photographs Printed Directly from the Original Negatives*. Although Emerson is included, all of the images of him are derived from pictures known to have been taken by photographers other than Brady. Meserve's Brady collection went to the National Portrait Gallery, Washington, D.C., which is the source for nearly all attributions of Emerson to Brady, probably on the assumption that if the image appeared in *Historical Portraits*, then it was by Brady.

If Brady did, in fact, take the photograph in either his New York or Washington studio, there are a fair number of opportunities when it might have occurred. Since no documentation of Emerson's sitting for Brady has surfaced, any conjecture would be unfounded at this point. Without more information, no determination can be made about whether or not this photograph was taken by Brady or by someone else, or about when or where it was taken.

BEFORE 1862

Undated silhouette

Courtesy Concord Museum

Silhouettes of, from left to right, Amos Bronson Alcott, Emerson, and Henry David Thoreau, as identified by Ellery Channing. Dated by the Concord Museum "1845–1860" and described as "May have been made at the end of the 19th century for Boston publisher Henry Oscar Houghton [1823–1895], who published a set of authors' images." A search of Houghton, Mifflin's catalogues failed to find silhouettes for sale, and the firm's *Portraits and Biographical Sketches of Twenty American Authors* includes only engravings.

1874[?]

Bust of Emerson in 1874[?] by John Crookshanks King

From the May 1903 *Critic*, described as "modelled in 1854."

Born in Scotland, John Crookshanks King (1806–1882) came to the United States in 1829, worked as a mechanic in New Orleans, Cincinnati, and Louisville, took up sculpting, and moved to Boston, where he died. He made busts of Daniel Webster, John Quincy Adams, and Louis Agassiz, as well as of Emerson.

On 4 November 1857, Emerson wrote a letter of introduction for King to Thomas Carlyle in which he referred to King's busts of Samuel Hoar and Daniel Webster. King does not appear elsewhere in Emerson's letters or journals, nor did Emerson's family refer to Emerson's sitting for a bust by King, suggesting that King may have made the bust without benefit of Emerson's presence.

As documented in the *Catalogue of Oil-Paintings, Water-Colors, and Engravings, in the Art Exposition, of the Twelfth Exhibition of the Massachusetts Charitable Mechanic Association, in Boston, 1874*, King submitted his bust of Emerson, in plaster. Emerson busts by Thomas Ridgeway Gould and Martin Milmore were also entered in that exhibition.

Sanborn described King's bust as "unspeakably bad."

Note one: CFPL has a photograph of this bust, owned in 1982 by Henry Fredette of Fitchburg, Massachusetts, indicating that it measures 29" x 18". A plaster cast of the bust, advertised in *Catalogue of Plaster Reproductions . . . Made and For Sale by P. P. Caproni and Brother*, is also 29" high.

Note two: According to John McAleer, who dates the bust as being sculpted in 1854, Emerson said of King's bust, "It looks as harmless as a parsnip." Both Samuel Howe and Daniel Chester French used the same phrase without identifying the sculptor to whom Emerson referred: Howe related a comment Emerson "made at one time of the work of a brother sculptor: 'It looks as harmless as a parsnip,'" and French recalled that of "another bust that had been made of him . . . he said: 'It looks as harmless as a parsnip.'"

1900[?]

Bust of Emerson in 1900[?] by Sidney H. Morse

This bust was unveiled at the Second Church as part of its observances, and appeared in *The Second Church in Boston*.

In a 5 February 1982 letter to David Emerson, Walter Royal Jones Jr. wrote of this bust:

> While [the Rev. Levi Moore] Powers was serving the Church of The Messiah, in Buffalo, N.Y., he met the Boston sculptor, Sidney Morse, who although ill,

was working on a bust of Ralph Waldo Emerson. Morse died before the work was complete, but Powers had obtained permission to have a number of casts made. This was in 1903 or 1904, I think.

Six copies were made. One was given to Edward Emerson . . . Powers said that Edward Emerson thought highly of the work, saying (I quote Powers) "that even in its unfinished condition it is much better than any thing in clay or marble of his father, except Morse's statuet [*sic*] bust so familiar to lovers of Emerson."

According to Jones the six copies were dispersed as follows: in addition to the one given to Edward Emerson, others were given to Ernest Howard Crosby, the philanthropist Joseph Fels, the library of St. Lawrence University, the Buffalo Historical Society, and the last to the "new High School in Haverhill, Mass., at the time Powers left that city." He added that the Haverhill copy had been lost and the Buffalo copy "deteriorated and was discarded."

A photograph of this bust *in situ* is included as the frontispiece to William Taylor Newton's *Emersoniana*, compiled in 1907 by Newton, in an original photograph by Baldwin Coolidge:

Sanborn believed "Morse's reduced bust, at Concord, is unlucky in pose and expression; the full bust is better, as I remember it."

Joel Myerson and Leslie Perrin Wilson 103

N.D.

Undated painting

This appeared in color on the front of the dust jacket of Carlos Baker, *Emerson Among the Eccentrics*, where it was identified on the rear flap as "Portrait of Ralph Waldo Emerson." It now appears as part of the Metropolitan Museum of Art's digital collections as "Portrait of a Man," no artist given, and dated "1800–1850." The picture is definitely not of Emerson.

The image originally appeared in *Life in America* as "Courtesy of Chester Dale Collection." There it is identified as being Emerson and described as an oil painting attributed to Thomas Sully (1783–1872), measuring 30" x 25".

Appendix B
Unlocated Images of Emerson

This appendix contains information about images of Emerson which have not yet been located.

1848

Emerson mentioned in his journal of May 1848 "M. Lehmann, in Paris, who made a crayon sketch of my head." Henri Lehmann (1814–1882) was a German-born French portrait painter.

He was a friend of Marie de Flavigny, Comtesse d'Agoult (1805–1876), companion of Franz Liszt, and known as the writer "Daniel Stern." The sketch of Emerson's head was done at her request and apparently she retained it. Emerson also had this journal comment in 1848: "The artists found in my face the Indian type."

Alexander Ireland reported that, while Emerson was in Paris, James Oswald Murray "made a crayon sketch of Emerson, which is in the possession of the present writer."

1852

Caroline Davis Wilson (1810–1890) had written Emerson as early as 3 December 1850 about making a bust of him, and in July 1852, she suggested either he call on her at Cambridge or she could come to Concord, which she did by mid-August. While in Cincinnati in 1852, Emerson wrote home on 15 December that "Mrs Wilson goes on, ah me! with the bust," and on the eighteenth, he wrote that he saw her "daily." In June 1853 Elizabeth Palmer Peabody urged Emerson to see Wilson so that she could make changes in her bust of him. As late as 1867, Emerson sent her a copy of *May-Day and Other Pieces*.

According to *Artists in Ohio, 1787–1900*, when with a party including Emerson visiting the Mammoth Cave in Kentucky in June 1850, Wilson "stopped the riverboat, scooped up some soft clay, and modeled a bust of Emerson on the spot; a bronze version of it was made in 1852." Emerson did list Wilson as among the party but made no mention of the impromptu sculpture.

1855

The *Boston Evening Transcript* advertised on 29 January 1855 that a "photographic likeness of Emerson" was for sale at Masury & Silsbee, 299½ Washington Street, Boston, "of the size and style of their extensive series of portraits of distinguished men."

1858

Ellen Emerson wrote her cousin Haven on 7 May 1858 that "Father is also sitting to Mr. Wight in Boston, who is taking an oil-painting of him, but that, on which I had set my heart, Father says is 'swinish-looking.'"

Moses Wight (1827–1895) was a Boston-based portrait artist. In 1872 his "studio was burned with many valuable canvases," one of them possibly being of Emerson.

1866

Emerson wrote Harrison Gray Otis Blake (1816–1898) of Worcester, Massachusetts, and a friend of Henry David Thoreau's, on 31 December 1866 that if he was to "stay for the affliction of a photographer," he might as well "stay over a train in the morning."

1868

Ellen Emerson wrote to Gisela von Arnim Grimm on 2 March 1868 that she was sending a picture of her father, "a little tin-type which was taken with his collar off for an artist who is cutting a cameo of him, and which is remarkably good." Later, on the thirteenth, she asks her brother Edward, "Where are Father's tin-types?"

1873

Rusk reports having seen a "large Robert Crawshay photo dated April, 1873," showing Emerson "looking firm and with a good deal of hair, but considerably aged."

Robert Thompson Crawshay (1817–1879) headed a major ironworks but took up photography after an illness left him deaf and unable to listen to music, his first passion. Emerson had met his father when visiting England in 1848.

1879

Ellen Emerson wrote to Gisela von Arnim Grimm on 22 January 1880, while enclosing a picture of the Emerson family at Thanksgiving (see 1879), that in

> October of this year, when the leaves were falling, a photographer came, and made a picture [of the house] which seems to me perfect . . . . My donkey is tied to the horse-post, and Father is on the way to the garden to look at his pear trees. His pruning-shears were in his right hand, which doesn't show. You will think it a pity to put him in a place where he looks so small, and my donkey larger; but each had to be in a *natural* place, and Father is standing where he passes ten times a day, there could be no other place, out of doors, more his own than that path.

1829

Painting of Emerson in 1829 by Sarah Goodridge

In his account book for 1875, Emerson notes "Pd Photographs and ~~instrument~~ frame; to be brought next week of Ellen Tucker E's miniature 3.50 10.30" and "Paid Whipple's successors, in Temple St. for copy of Ellen Tucker's miniature" (25, 27 April, "Account Book 1872–1882," HL, MS Am 1280H [112h]).

According to . . . 1829: *OFL*, 176.

"Miniatures of . . . perfect": MHS, Ms N-251 (138).

"Ellen Tucker pin": *LetETE*, 1:226.

"I paint . . . best": *OFL*, 23–24.

"Thine Eyes Still Shined": *The Poetry Notebooks of Ralph Waldo Emerson*, ed. Ralph H. Orth, Albert J. von Frank, et al. (Columbia: University of Missouri Press, 1986), 27.

"neither Mrs. . . . been": "Portraits," 453.

"a note . . . time": *OFL*, 176.

Locations: painting: unknown; (A) ambrotype: HL, bMS Am 1280.235 (706.1) (image 2¼" x 1¾"); (B) photograph: unknown.

Note one: Although Ellen Tucker refers to a "red morroco case," the case currently housing image (A) is brown.

Note two: The gold matting on image (A) is blindstamped "Sydney Miller, Artist, Nashua [New Hampshire]" at the top left and top right.

1843

Painted silhouette of Emerson in about 1843

(Boston: Cupples, Upham, 1887). Haskins also reproduces undated silhouettes of Edward Bliss Emerson (facing 87) and Charles Chauncy Emerson (facing 92); in the "List of Illustrations" in *J*, 3, the silhouette of Edward is dated 1827, and in the same list in *J*, 4, the silhouette of Charles is dated "about 1834" (both [xvii]).

Location: Bush (image: 16¾" x 12¾").

Note: An unsigned handwritten label on the back of the frame states the image is of brother William, not Waldo, Emerson.

1844

Miniatures of Emerson in 1844 painted by Caroline Neagus Hildreth

"Will you . . . I am?": *L*, 7:598.

"sat for . . . beau": *L*, 3:255–256.

"Mrs. Hildreth . . . 6 December: "Account Book 1840–1844," HL, MS Am 1280H (112b); the daughters' image is at Bush and is reproduced at: <http://www.concordlibrary.org/scollect/Emerson_Celebration/Em_Con_71.html> (accessed 23 August 2015).

"this plight . . . September": *L*, 7:609.

"Mrs Hildreth has . . . them": *L*, 3:264.

"new miniature . . . side": *L*, 3:270, 272.

"must judge of it." *through* "I am . . . expression": *L*, 3:275.

"miniatures": 10 January 1845, "Account Book 1845–1849," HL, MS Am 1280H (112c).

"Photogravure" *and* "a miniature . . . Hildreth": *J*, 1:xxvii.

"a pleasing . . . strength": "Portraits," 455.

One of the miniatures was loaned to Rufus Wilmot Griswold for engraving by John Sartain in the former's *Prose Writers of America* but was not returned until April 1847. William liked it enough to ask Waldo for a copy ([Philadelphia: Carey and Hart, 1847], facing 440; see *L*, 3:371, 8:26, 71–72, 78, and 5 April 1847, 8:116; 30 [March 1847], MHS Ms N-251 [432]). This image is:

Hildreth kept working on the miniature retained by Emerson throughout 1852 in order to improve it (see *L*, 4:298, 306, 308, 309, 413, 417).

Locations: miniatures: first: unknown; second: Bush (4½" x 3½"; back: "Ralph Waldo Emerson | Aged 42 yrs | Painted by Miss Negus [*sic*] afterward Mrs. Richard Hildreth | Owned by [Mrs.] William H. Forbes | Milton | Mass.").

1846

Daguerreotype of Emerson in 1846 by Alfred Sands Southworth

As early . . . of Emerson: *CEC*, 307.

"There is . . . forbid!": 4 August 1841, *The Carlyle Letters Online*, ed. Brent Kinser (Durham: Duke University Press, 2007); accessed 25 March 2014.

journal entries: see *JMN*, 8:115–116, 125–126, 139–140, 142.

"I was . . . sketcher": *CEC*, 398.

"last Monday . . . better": *CEC*, 400.

studio ledger: *Young America: The Daguerreotypes of Southworth & Hawes*, ed. Grant B. Romer and Brian Wallis (New York: International Center for Photography; Rochester, N.Y.: George Eastman House; Göttinger: Steidl, 2005), 281.

"a very . . . style": *L*, 8:83.

"this poor . . . in this": *CEC*, 404.

"I tried . . . him": "Diary for January-March 1850," 273–275, HL, MS Am 1130.12 (19).

"professed to . . . can": *CEC*, 419.

"from a . . . life": Ireland, x; image facing [246].

Emerson paid Southworth (1811–1894) one dollar on 15 June 1846 "to send first miniature to England," and four dollars the same day "for second miniature." On the twenty-fourth, he paid Southworth $12.50 for "Daguerreotype miniature in an extra case." The studio records confirm that Emerson purchased "three miniatures of the quarter-plate size for $16.00" ("Account Book 1845–1849," HL, MS Am 1280H [112c]; *Young America*, 326).

When the image was reproduced as the frontispiece to *Nature, Addresses, and Lectures*, the first volume in the Riverside Edition of Emerson's *Works*, the credit line read "The portrait . . . was etched by Mr. Schoff from a photographic copy (kindly furnished by Mr. Alexander Ireland, of Manchester, England) of a daguerreotype taken in 1847 or 1848, probably in England." When it appeared as the frontispiece in *W*, 1, it was described in the "List of Illustrations" as "From a daguerreotype in 1847, now in the possession of the Carlyle family, England." But when it appeared as the frontispiece in *J*, 7, it was described in the list of illustrations as a "Photogravure" of "a daguerreotype taken for Carlyle in May, 1846" ([Boston: Houghton, Mifflin, 1883], iv; [xi]; [xxi]).

Locations: daguerreotype: unknown; CDV-size paper prints: (A) CFPL (5½" x 3¾"; this appears to have been photographed from the original as indicated by scratch marks such as are visible when seeing images on glass); (B) Carlyle House, London (4¼" x 2½").

Note: Ellen wrote her sister Edith on 5 July 1872 regarding the image sent to Carlyle that "[t]here are no copies of the daguerreotype, they were distributed years ago" (*LetETE*, 1:670).

1846

Crayon and chalk portrait of Emerson in the fall of 1846 by Eastman Johnson

"complied with . . . Maine": *1846: Portrait of a Nation* (Washington: Smithsonian Institution Press, 1996), 176: no evidence is presented for the date, which cannot be confirmed in any of Emerson's or Longfellow's published letters or journals.

"the exact . . . unclear": *Eastman Johnson: Painting America* (New York: Brooklyn Museum of Art and Rizzoli, 1999), 13–14.

"about 1846": *J*, 5, [xix].

Longfellow sat . . . friends: Samuel Longfellow, *Life of Henry Wadsworth Longfellow*, 2 vols. (Boston: Ticknor, 1886), 2:57n; Carbone and Hills, 13.

"the poorest": "Portraits," 468; the other crayon portraits are by Rowse (1858).

"No one . . . than that": Edgar French, "An American Portrait Painter of Three Historical Epochs," *World's Work* 13 (December 1906): 8317.

Location: Longfellow National Historical Site, Cambridge, Mass. (21" x 19").

Note: A CDV was made of this image, probably by the Longfellow family: the copy at HNE was donated by a Longfellow descendant:

Locations: Berg (483510; f: blank; b: John A. Whipple, 297 Washington St., Boston, an address he moved to in 1865 [*Encyclopedia of Nineteenth-Century Photography*, ed. John Hannavy (New York: Routledge, 2008), 1495]); HNE (b: John A. Whipple, 297 Washington St.).

1848

Daguerreotype of Emerson in 1848

(New York: Oxford University Press, 1936), frontispiece, credited "Courtesy of Mrs. Louis Pirrson" (wife of a Yale professor):

Emerson purchased "visiting Cards" for one shilling in London on 26 October 1847 (*JMN*, 10:409), but it is unclear whether these were for cartes-de-visite (or which image appeared on them) or blank cards on which he could write his current name and address. Joel Myerson has one of the latter on which Emerson wrote "Mr Emerson | 142 Strand," the address of his publisher, Chapman and Hall.

Location: daguerreotype: Ralph Waldo Emerson Collection, Yale Collection of American Literature, Beinecke Rare Book and Manuscript Library (YCA MSS 212; 5" x 4").

Note: Emerson stayed: *CEC*, 446*n*3; von Frank, 1:524.

"gave this . . . family": "A New Portrait of Emerson," typescript, Yale, YCAL MSS 212, box 1, folder 36.

"I do . . . together": [Thomas Sadler], "Carlyle and Neuberg," *Macmillan's Magazine* 50 (August 1884): 280; *L*, 8:168.

1848

Oil painting of Emerson in 1848 by David Scott

They were introduced: William B. Scott, *Memoir of David Scott* (Edinburgh: Adam & Charles Black, 1850), 293.

"a sort . . . persons": 22[?] February, *L*, 4:18, 20.

"guarded, and . . . hard": Scott, 299.

According to Bronson Alcott: "Journal January–March 1850," 19 February, 273, HL, MS Am 1130.12 (19).

"Tis very . . . images": *L*, 6:86–87; 9:353.

Ultimately . . . 1873: "The Library: Report of the Town Committee," *Annual Reports of the Selectmen and Other Officers of the Town of Concord, from March 1, 1873, to March 1, 1874* (Boston: Tolman & White, 1874), 46.

"David Scott . . . of hope": "Speech of Edward Waldo Emerson," *The Centenary of the Birth of Ralph Waldo Emerson As Observed in Concord May 25 1903 Under the Direction of the Social Circle in Concord* (Cambridge, Mass.: Riverside Press for the Social Circle in Concord, 1903), 126–27.

"a very . . . to Emerson": *Emerson at Home and Abroad* (Boston: James R. Osgood, 1882), 328–329.

"best of . . . dark": "Portraits," 449–450.

Location: CFPL (oil on panel; 48" x 36"; presented by Ebenezer Rockwood Hoar, Elizabeth Hoar, and Reuben N. Rice, 1873).

Note: The Jenkins Company offered for sale what was described as Scott's preliminary watercolor (7" x 5") for his painting of Emerson in catalogue 115, 1978:

Location: unknown.

1848[?]

Photograph of Emerson in 1848[?]

First published: *CEC*, facing 52.

Location: HL, bMS Am 1280.235 (706.3b) (stiff paper print, 6¼" x 4").

1850s[?]

Drawings of Emerson by Harriot Appleton Curtis

Location: HNE (9" x 8").

Note: The images originally appeared on the recto of the sheet, the one on the left here at the top left, the one on the right here, upside down at the top right. The images have been cropped and repositioned for the current entry.

1850

Drawing of Emerson in 1850 by Fredrika Bremer

America of . . . Bremer: ed. Adolph B. Benson (New York: American-Scandinavian Foundation, 1924), 42–46, 66, which reproduces Bremer's drawing of Emerson facing 311.

Signe Alice . . . *1849–1851*: (Philadelphia, American Swedish Historical Foundation, 1955), which reproduces the sketch on 43.

Emerson mentions . . . 16 March 1850: *L*, 4:176–177, 8:285, 4:184*n*.

"Her talent . . . drawn": "Diary for January–March 1850," 2–3, HL, MS Am 1130.12 (19).

"portrait of . . . like": *The George Eliot Letters*, ed. Gordon S. Haight, 9 vols. (New Haven: Yale University Press, 1954–1978), 1:367.

Location: Kungliga biblioteket (National Library of Sweden), Stockholm (7¾" x 4½"; pasted in sketchbook nr1 [HS Acc 2008/103:3]).

1854

Daguerreotypes of Emerson in 1854 by Josiah Johnson Hawes

IMAGE (A1)

"From a . . . 1854": 28:265.

The Centenary . . . Emerson: *The Centenary of the Birth of Ralph Waldo Emerson . . .* (Cambridge, Mass.: Riverside Press for the Social Circle in Concord, 1903).

"from a . . . reproduced": *W*, 2:[v].

"Daguerreotypes": *LetETE*, 1:56.

date of autumn 1856: "A Famous Photographer and His Sitters," *Demorest's Family Magazine* 34 (April 1898): 134.

"'a magnificent . . . daguerreotypists": *The Letters of William Lloyd Garrison*, ed. Louis Ruchames, 6 vols. (Cambridge, Mass.: Harvard University Press, 1961–1981), 4:413–414.

"though I . . . artists": *L*, 8:516.

1857 broadside: (Boston: C. H. Brainard, 1857), copies at Athenæum and MHS, both 22" x 18", and Kenneth Walter Cameron, "C. H. Brainard and the Grozelier Portraits of Emerson," *American Transcendental Quarterly* no. 36, part 1 (Fall 1977): 48–51, esp. 50.

"this day published": 27:7.

Sara Peters: *American Portrait Miniatures in the Metropolitan Museum of Art*, ed. Carrie Rebora Barratt and Lori Zabar (New York: Metropolitan Museum of Art; New Haven: Yale University Press, 2010), 231.

fundraiser: suggested by Albert J. von Frank, email to Myerson, 16 August 2015.

IMAGE (A2)

Engel . . . *Emersons*: (Los Angeles: Times-Mirror, 1941), facing 138.

"the photograph . . . 1854": Engel, 138.

IMAGE (B)

"a large . . . send you that": *LetETE*, 1:465.

24 February 1868: *L*, 6:6.

"I have . . . visit": *Memoirs of Anne C. L. Botta*, [ed. Vincenzo Botta] (New York: J. Selwin

Tait and Sons, 1894), 296–297; the "other" photograph may be Image (A1).

"one of Southworths": *L*, 9:330.

"carrying" *and* "the Southworth head": *L*, 6:56.

"Southworth's large photograph": *JMN*, 16:260, and see *L*, 6:190–191.

Sanborn wrote . . . 1850: "Portraits," 456.

"reduced from . . . before": Ireland, x, facing [140].

Bronson Alcott: *Ralph Waldo Emerson: An Estimate of His Character in Prose and Verse* (Boston: A. Williams, 1882).

"well-known" *and* "made, Mr. Hawes . . . me": 2 vols. (Boston: Houghton, Mifflin, 1887), 1: frontispiece, v-vi.

"a 'counterfeit . . . inviting": "Cabot's Memoir of Emerson," *Unitarian Review* 28 (November 1887): 417.

Also . . . '1854'": *W*, 9: [xviii].

Entries in Emerson's account book in 1868 bear out the interest shown in this image and confirm his daughter's statement: on 25 January he paid one dollar for a "head" to send a friend; on 17 March he paid "Hawes for 3 photographs large size 3.00"; and in March he also paid "Hawes for 12 cartes de visite photographs of my head 4.00." The copy of image (B) at the George Eastman Museum, Rochester, N.Y., is inscribed on the back: "copied (by J. J. Hawes) from a daguerreotype portrait by A. S. Southworth & J. J. Hawes" ("Account Book 1865–1872," HL, MS Am 1280H [112g]).

Locations: (A1) daguerreotype: HL, bMS Am 2911; (A2) original: unknown; (B) large photograph: Carlyle House, London (12" x 8"), George Eastman Museum, Rochester, N.Y. (1981:2711:0001; 13" x 9"; written on back: "copied (by J. J. Hawes) from a daguerreotype portrait by A. S. Southworth & J. J. Hawes . . . print by J. J. Hawes"), JM (21½" x 17½") [and see *Note* below]; others: facing right: Bostonian (NEL 2304; CDV: b: J. Hawes), CFPL (cabinet: "A[lfred]. Munroe"), National Portrait Gallery, London (S.NPG.81.25; carbon print photograph cabinet card, ca. 1875 [after ca. 1856 daguerreotype] with "J. J. Hawes, 10 Tremont Row" at the bottom);

facing left: JM (CDV 13; b: Warren's Studio, 289 Washington St, "under the superintendence of Mr. S. B. Heald"), JM (CDV 30; b: blank).

Note: Three large prints of image (B), all facing right, have been noted for sale:

Cedric L. Robinson (catalogues 173, #256, and 182, #67) reproduced a "Photographic Print 22" x 17½" on contemporary mount board . . . . Early typescript label attached to a clipped portion of original backing paper: 'Reverend David Greene Haskins and Mrs. Haskins. On their Golden Wedding Day [1892]. With best wishes from their cousins Ellen T. Emerson and Edward Waldo Emerson." Robinson suggests, "It could also have been produced for the Emerson children by Hawes around 1890. Magazine articles of the late 1880s reported that the then elderly Hawes from time to time still made albumen print enlargements of his old daguerreotype portraits. This later possibility is less likely however, as, if the original daguerreotype was then extant, so late in Hawes' career, it would have been passed on to the museums which acquired Hawes' collection from his son" (catalogue 173).

Charles Agvent's web catalogue <www. charlesagvent.com/shop/agvent/011969.html> (accessed 24 April 2014) reproduced a 12½" x 8½" image ("matted and framed to an overall size of 20" x 15""); on "the rear of the frame are two labels from Holman's Print Shop of Boston, circa 1940, on which is stated the following: 'This photograph was in J. J. Hawes' studio at the time of his death and was stored with the rest of the contents until 1934, when it came to us for sale. It is a photographic copy of a daguerreotype portrait made by Mr. Hawes in the 1840's. The negative was a collodion-process plate ('wet plate'). This print could have been made as late as the 1890's, but more probably dates from the 1880's. When Mr. Hawes made the copy of the daguerreotype is not known.'"

A signed copy was listed in Christie's sale 3750 on 12 June 2015, item 78, as an "albumen photograph . . . 11¼ x 8⅜ in. Unidentifed photographer, ca. 1859. Mounted on card, boldly signed by Emerson along lower edge of the card." This is the image reproduced as (B) above.

MID-1850S

Emerson in the mid-1850s

Locations: (A) JM (CDV 16; b: blank); (B) JM (CDV 28; b: "Photographic Gallery of Harwell and Hancock, 28½ Main St., Memphis"); (C) Bodleian Library, Oxford University (John Johnson Collection; CDV: b: E. and H. T. Anthony, 501 Broadway, New York; after 1852, when the firm was founded), JM (CDV 10; b: E. and H. T. Anthony, 501 Broadway), National Archives (BA-1620; b: unknown; dated 1860–1865).

1857[?] AND 1858[?]

Daguerreotypes of Emerson in 1857[?] and 1858[?] by Southworth and Hawes

IMAGE (A)

date of 1857: *The Spirit of Fact: The Daguerreotypes of Southworth & Hawes, 1843–1862* (Boston: David R. Godine, 1976), plate 3.

"Emerson appears . . . 1858–59": *Facing the Light*, 314.

IMAGE (B)

taken from its case: *Facing the Light*, 141.

"faithful to . . . fun": "Portraits," 455, where he erroneously captioned the picture as "From a photograph by Black, about 1860."

Literature & Photography: Literature & Photography: Interactions 1840–1990, ed. Jane M. Rabb (Albuquerque: University of New Mexico Press, 1995), 17.

A Curious & Ingenious Art: Melissa Banta, *A Curious & Ingenious Art: Reflections on Daguerreotypes at Harvard* (Iowa City: University of Iowa Press, 2000), 98.

"ca. 1850": *Facing the Light*, 141.

First reproduced . . . *Ancestors:* (Boston: Cupples, Upham, 1887).

"From a . . . family": *W*, 3: frontispiece, [v].

"From a . . . Grozelier": *W*, 6: frontispiece, [iii].

Locations: (A) whole plate daguerreotype: HNE (1920.321; gift of the Hawes family); (B1) photograph of daguerreotype without case: HNE; (B2) quarterplate daguerreotype: HL, bMS Am 1280.235 (706.2), size of image 3½" x 2½".

CDVs and cabinets: BPL (13_05_000902; CDV: b: J. W. Black, 333 Washington Street, where he was between 1875 and 1901 [Steele and Polito, 31]), CFPL (CDV: b: blank), JM (cabinet 7; b: handwritten "Return to F[rancis]. J[ackson]. Garrison" [William Lloyd Garrison's son]), MHS (Photo Collection 20, box 5, folder 39; CDV-size paper print pasted in album and attributed to Black), Smithsonian Institution, Archives of American Art, (DSI-AAA, 5676 [CDV attributed to Black and dated between 1860 and 1870]; b: unknown).

Note one: Grozelier: This was printed by J[ohn]. H[enry]. Bufford's of Boston, and published in New York by M. Knœdler, 366 Broadway, and in London and Paris by Goupil. The Library of Congress copy was received 21 January 1860.

"especially liked . . . remain": Nathaniel Hawthorne, *Biographical Stories* (Cambridge, Mass.: Houghton, Mifflin, 1890), advertisements, [10], following 82.

Note two: Attribution: James Wallace Black: M. Susan Barger and William B. White, *The Daguerreotype: Nineteenth-Century Technology and Science* (Washington, D.C.: Smithsonian, 1991), 88; Steele and Polito, 31.

1858

Crayon sketches of Emerson in 1858 by Samuel Worcester Rowse

IMAGE (A)

"Rowse said . . . strength": *JMN*, 14:203–204.

"I think . . . one": *L*, 5:114.

"picture is . . . again": *LetETE*, 1:141–142.

"threw aside . . . 1882": "Portraits," 456; see Amos Bronson Alcott, *Sonnets and Canzonets* (Boston: Roberts Brothers, 1882), facing 107 (limited printing only).

"From a . . . satisfied": [v].

"Pd S. W. . . . 5.00": "Account Book 1853–1859," HL, MS Am 1280H (112e).

Rowse, commissioned . . . of Emerson'": "Samuel Worcester Rowse," *The Early Years of the Saturday Club, 1855–1870* (Boston: Houghton Mifflin, 1918), 389.

"though a . . . good": *J*, 9:154*n*.

"Rowse's crayon . . . mouth": *The Early Years of the Saturday Club*, 389.

"a certain . . . simper": "Portraits," 456.

IMAGE (B)

"At Williams . . . possible": 5:374.

"one of . . . characteristic": "Reviews and Literary Notices," *Atlantic Monthly* 3 (May 1859): 654.

"This bust . . . last": *LetLdE*, 210.

Emerson sent . . . January 1859: *L*, 5:133.

"another, after . . . respectable": *L*, 5:444.

"I think . . . by it": 28 December 1858, *The Correspondence of Arthur Hugh Clough*, ed. Frederick L. Mulhauser, 2 vols. (Oxford: Clarendon Press, 1957), 2:561.

"reproduced the . . . them": *Talks with Emerson* (New York: Baker and Taylor, 1890), 122.

"photograph" and "That is . . . done": *Reminiscences of Ednah Dow Cheney* (Boston: Lee & Shepard, 1902), 133.

For comments by Sanborn and Edward Waldo Emerson, see the description of image (A) above. Reproduced in *W*, 6, facing 167. For more on Rowse, see Patricia Hills, "Gentle Portraits of the Longfellow Era: The Drawings of Samuel Worcester Rowse," *Drawing* 2 (March-April 1981): 121–126.

Emerson entered into his account book on 12 November 1858, "Pd Williams and Everett, for 6 copies of photograph of my head by Rowse." Later, in 1865 he "pd Allen photographer for 3 Cartes de visite of Rowse's head of RWE .75" and "pd Allen photographer for 3 Cartes de visite of Rowse's head of RWE .75" ("Account Book 1853–1859," HL, MS Am 1280H [112e]; 26 December, "Account Book 1865–1872," HL, MS Am 1280H [112g]).

Rowse may have exhibited this at the Boston Athenæum in 1859: he is given as the artist of "R. W. Emerson," listed in the paintings section that also contains crayon portraits (Boston Athenæum, *Catalogue of the Thirty-Third Exhibition of Paintings and Statuary . . . 1859* [Boston: Prentiss, Sawyer, 1859], 11, item 36).

Locations: (A) original: unknown; CDVs: Athenæum (AA.5.4.Eme.r., no. 2; b: Allen, 24 Temple Place, where he worked between 1869 and 1873 [Steele and Polito, 24]), CFPL (f: James Wallace Black; b: blank), JM (CDV 27; b: blank); (B): original: Bush (16¾" x 12¾"); copies: CFPL (CDV by E[ward]. L. Allen), HNE (8½" x 6¼" photograph "Drawn by S. W. Rowse   Photographed by S. Masury" and copyrighted 1858 by Williams & Everett).

Note: Schoff: An engraving: ed. Charles Eliot Norton, 2 vols. (Boston: James R. Osgood, 1883), 2: frontispiece.

"Schoff has . . . it": letter to James Elliot Cabot, 30 June 1883, HL, bMS Am 1280.226 (272).

"a remarkable . . . have": "Editor's Easy Chair," *Harper's New Monthly Magazine* 59 (June 1879): 139.

"although it . . . intellect—?": "The Correspondence of Carlyle and Emerson," *Christian Register* 62 (15 March 1883): 164.

larger version of the Emerson image: a copy on paper is at the National Portrait Gallery, London (NPG.79.157), one on rice paper is at JM; in both the image measures 9½" x 6⅛".

LATE 1850S

Emerson in the late 1850s

IMAGE (A)

Anthony moved: advertisement, [John C.] Gobright and [Hodgson] Pratt, *The Union Sketch-Book: A Reliable Guide, Exhibiting the History and Business Resources of the Leading Mercantile and Manufacturing Firms of New York . . .* (New York: Pudney & Russell, 1860), 145.

"From a . . . 1856": "Portraits," 460.

"From a . . . 1859": *W*, 7: frontispiece, [v].

He did head west: von Frank, 2:717–721, 743–747, 782, 806–811.

IMAGE (C)

Sonnets and Canzonets: (Boston: Roberts Brothers, 1882), facing 105 (limited printing only).

Talks with . . . Emerson: (New York: Baker & Taylor, 1890), frontispiece.

Locations: (A) CFPL (CDV: b: Anthony), JM (CDV 14; b: Anthony); (B) JM (CDV 25; b: Anthony); (C) Bush (large ambrotype), CFPL (CDV: b: blank), Gilda Lehrman Institute of American History (GLC0514; CDV: f: "Whipple, Washington St., Boston"; b: blank).

Note: Thomas Murphy Johnston (1836–1869) made a drawing of this image, which was published in Boston by C. H. Brainard in 1858:

The image is signed in the stone and copyrighted in 1858. According to the *Liberator* of 10 December 1858, Brainard "just published a very admirable and life-like portrait of Mr. Emerson, after the style of . . . Grozelier, though by another artist, T. M. Johnston." In using this image as the frontispiece for his *Emerson as a Poet*, Joel Benton stated Brainard's "admirable lithograph . . . had its origin in a photograph owned by Theodore Parker, and which was Mr. Parker's favorite picture of this author. To many others, also, no other portrait of Emerson recalls him so perfectly in his best attitude, as he was in his prime" ("Portrait of Ralph Waldo Emerson," 199; [Boston: M. L. Holbrook, 1882], 8: also used as the frontispiece in the 1883 edition by M. F. Mansfield & A. Wessels of New York).

This, in turn, served as the basis for a carte-de-visite published in 1860:

Ralph Waldo Emerson.

Locations: Brainard image: Athenæum (C 5.4 Eme.r.1858; 19" x 16" [image area 15" x 12½"]); CDV: CFPL (b: blank); JM (CDV 29; b: blank).

LATE 1850S

Emerson in the late 1850s

Taber was a partner: *New Bedford Massachusetts: Its History, Industries, Institutions and Attractions*, ed. William L. Sayer (New Bedford: Mercury, 1889), 194.

Locations: Berg (albumen print, 4" x 2½", pasted on a scrapbook page), JM (CDV 11; b: blank), JM (CDV 26; b: blank), JM (CDV 35; b: Taber).

1858

William James Stillman, The Philosophers' Camp in the Adirondacks *(1858)*

"[T]his image . . . seer": 2 vols. (Boston: Houghton Mifflin, 1901), 1:256.

Autograph Centenary Edition: 9: facing 184.

Stephen L. Dyson: (Albany: State University of New York Press, 2014), 85.

James Schlett: (Ithaca: Cornell University Press, 2015), dust jacket.

Edward Emerson's key: (Boston: Houghton Mifflin, 1918), following 170.

Location: CFPL (20⅛" x 30"; oil on canvas, 1858; from the bequest of Ebenezer Rockwood Hoar, 1895).

Note: Key: CFPL (13⅜" x 22¾"; pencil on paper; presented by Edward Waldo Emerson, 1895).

1858

Emerson with Edith and Edward in 1858

J, 9: facing 126.

photogravure from . . . lap: *J*, 9:[xxiii].

"He liked . . . us": (Boston: Houghton, Mifflin, 1889), 170.

Clough expressed a desire: Clough to Emerson, 4 July, *The Correspondence of Arthur Hugh Clough*, ed. Frederick L. Mulhauser, 2 vols. (Oxford: Clarendon Press, 1957), 2:587.

"the best . . . taken": 2 March 1868, *LetETE*, 1:465.

Location: ambrotype: HL, bMS Am 2911; paper print: CFPL (4" x 3½").

1858[?]

Emerson in 1858[?]

IMAGE (A)

Silsbee and Case worked together: Steele and Polito, 121.

IMAGE (B)

"From an . . . 1858": *W*, 11: frontispiece, [xiii].

travel west: von Frank, 2:761, 744–747.

Locations: (A) Athenæum (AA.5.4.Eme.r., no. 3; CDV), CFPL (CDV), JM (CDV 18), MHS (Ms-N251.147; CDV); (B) ambrotype: unknown.

1859

Bust of Emerson in 1859 by Sidney H. Morse

"entered the . . . marble": James B. Elliott, "Sidney H. Morse," *Humanitarian Review* 3 (July 1905): 256.

"gained some . . . others": "The Free Religious Association," *New England Magazine* n.s. 28 (June 1903): 494.

"Morse's reduced . . . it": "Portraits," 468.

"From a . . . 1859": *W*, 4: frontispiece, [v].

Essays: First Series: (Boston: Houghton, Mifflin, 1883).

"Emerson's features . . . other": William C. Gore, "Letter from a Sculptor," *Inlander* 6 (October 1896): 4.

"seemed to . . . than I'": n.d., Rusk's notes.

Copies of Morse's bust: 3: advertisements following 488.

"a new . . . Edward Emerson": "Notes," *Pacific Unitarian* 2 (May 1894): 197.

The 15 May 1919 issue of the *Christian Register* included James K. Hosmer's "An Uncompromising Radical Church," which described the enshrinement of Morse's bust of Emerson when a church building for the First Unitarian Church of Minneapolis was constructed in 1886, but does not indicate the size of the bust (98:469).

Locations: small and large busts: unknown.

BETWEEN 1860 AND 1868

Emerson between 1860 and 1868 by James Wallace Black

IMAGE (A)

The peculiarly . . . pose: see Oliver Wendell Holmes, *Ralph Waldo Emerson* (Boston: Houghton, Mifflin, 1885), 360.

"a good . . . voice": "Portraits," 467.

"He came . . . manner": "Emerson's Lecture," *Howitt's Journal* 2 (11 December 1847): 370.

Black . . . 333 Washington Street: Steele and Polito, 31.

W placed it at 1857: 8: facing 178, and "List of Illustrations," [xviii].

Sanborn dated it at 1869: "Portraits," 455.

Note: Emerson wrote on 27 June 1861 to Herman Grimm, who had asked him on 25 October 1860 to "please send us a very good portrait of you," that "Ellen had inclosed in her letter some scrap of an effigy. But I am told that I shall yet have a better to send." Grimm wrote on 19 October 1867 that if Emerson would send a recent "portrait," he would "complete our collection of your portraits, of which we have quite a number." One of these could be image (A), which was used as the frontispiece to *Correspondence between Ralph Waldo Emerson and Herman Grimm* (*L*, 9:52; ed. Frederick William Holls [Boston: Houghton, Mifflin, 1903], 53, 75).

IMAGES (B)–(E)

"the next . . . person": *LetETE*, 1:465; see 1858 for "The Virgil Lesson."

John E. Tilton . . . 161 Washington Street: Steele and Polito, 163.

"a photograph by Black": "Portraits," 458.

"From a photograph . . . *Boston*": *Bookman* (London) 24 (June 1903): 102.

Black . . . 173 Washington Street: eBay #311372800326, accessed 8 June 2015; Steele and Polito, 31.

Locations: (A) Archives of American Art (DSI-AAA 5677; CDV: b: unknown), Collection of Ronald A. Bosco (cabinet: f: J. W. Black, 333 Washington Street; b: blank), Bostonian (34.37.3; CDV: b: blank), CFPL (CDV: b: Tilton and Black), JM (CDV 33 TK; b: Tilton and Black), HNE (CDV: b: Black, 173 Washington Street), MHS (Photo Collection 152.43; CDV: b: Tilton and Black), Collection of Joel Myerson (CDV: b: blank), Smithsonian (CDV: front: Black; b: unknown; dated between 1860 and 1870); (B) CFPL (CDV: b: blank); (C1) Athenæum (AA.5.4.Eme.r., no. 1; CDV: f: Tilton and Black; b: blank), CFPL (CDV: b: Tilton), JM (CDV 24; b: Tilton and Black), JM (CDV 20; b: "Black and Case, 168 and 173 Washington St., & 2 Downing's Block, Newport"), National Portrait Gallery,

London (NPG x14303; b: unknown; attributed to Black); (c2) George Eastman Museum, Rochester, N.Y. (1981.3027.0003; b: written in ink "Edith E. Forbes, R. W. E. aged about 56"); (c3) JM (CDV 9; b: Black and Case, Boston and Newport, R.I.); (D) JM (CDV 34 TK; b: Tilton and Black); (E) Athenæum (AA.5.4.Eme.r., no. 5; CDV: b: blank), JM (CDV 33; b: Tilton).

Note: Jeremiah Gurney: Christian A. Peterson, *Chaining the Sun: Portraits by Jeremiah Gurney* (Minneapolis: Minneapolis Institute of Arts, 1999], and <http://broadway.cas.sc.edu/content/studio-gurney-and-son> (accessed 19 September 2014).

Location: JM (CDV 19; b: Gurney).

1861

Bust of Emerson in 1861 by Thomas Ridgeway Gould

"kind proposal . . . 16 January: *L*, 9:3–4.

"made an . . . last": *LetLdE*, 210; see 1857 (B) for Rowse.

"pretty good": *LetETE*, 1:249.

"amateur bust": "Portraits," 468.

Emerson and Gould . . . homes: *L*, 5:328–329, 360, 410; *LetLdE*, 234.

"saw the . . . light": editor's summary, *L*, 5:329.

Gould's marble . . . 1865: <http://www.harvardartmuseums.org/art/305364> (accessed 21 August 2015).

Concord's plaster . . . Alcott: "The Library: Report of the Town Committee," *Annual Reports of the Selectmen and Other Officers of the Town of Concord, from March 1, 1873, to March 1, 1874, Being the Two Hundred and Thirty-Eighth Municipal Year* (Boston: Tolman & White, 1874), 47–48.

Alcott had . . . day: *The Letters of A. Bronson Alcott*, ed. Richard L. Herrnstadt (Ames: Iowa State University Press, 1969), 609.

A mounted . . . *Emerson*: (Cambridge, Mass.: privately printed, 1865).

"the best . . . extant": Alcott, *Letters*, 369.

Locations: (A) marble: Harvard University Portrait Collection, (B) plaster, CFPL.

Note: A painting of Emerson by Gould is listed in the Boston Athenæum's *Catalogue of the Fortieth Exhibition of Paintings and Statuary . . . 1864* (Boston: Fred Rogers, 1864), 17, item 227. This may be an erroneous entry for the bust.

1863 OR 1864

Emerson in 1863 or 1864 by Case and Getchell

Boston photographers . . . 299½ Washington Street: Steele and Polito, 39.

George M. . . . 1862: Steele and Polito, 121.

Black partnered . . . 1868: Steele and Polito, 31.

"Pd for . . . 1.50": "Account Book 1859–1865," HL, MS Am 1280H (112f).

Locations: Athenæum (C 5 Abo.1857; CDV: f: Case and Getchell; b: Case and Getchell, 299½ Washington Street), CFPL (CDV: b: Black, 173 Washington St., where he was in 1860–1874), Harvard University, Fine Arts Library (FAL87986; CDV: b: Silsbee, Case), HL, bMS Am 1280.235 [706.3c]; CDV-size picture pasted on cabinet card stock; f: Black, 333 Washington Street, where he was in 1875–1901; b: Black, dated in print 1895), JM (CDV 15; b: Black, 333 Washington Street), JM (CDV 35; f: Case and Getchell; b: Case and Getchell, 299½ Washington Street).

1864

Painting of Emerson in 1864 by William Henry Furness Jr.

"by a . . . yore": "Portraits," 451.

"Furness lives . . . malefactors": Francis B. Dedmond, "The Selected Letters of William Ellery Channing the Younger (Part Three)," *Studies in the American Renaissance 1991*, ed. Joel Myerson (Charlottesville: University Press of Virginia, 1991), 339.

The entire . . . 1866: *LetETE*, 1:371–372.

"an admirable picture": *L*, 10:57.

"a perpetual . . . prized": *L*, 9:359.

"At home . . . price": *L*, 10:57.

William Henry Furness replied . . . gratis: *Records of a Lifelong Friendship 1807–1882: Ralph Waldo Emerson and William Henry Furness*, ed. H[orace]. H[oward]. F[urness]. (Boston: Houghton Mifflin, 1910), 151, 154, 152n. The mezzotint engraving (6½" x 6") is described as "Private Plate," copyright 1871:

Courtesy of the Pennsylvania Academy of the Fine Arts, Philadelphia. Bequest of Dr. Paul J. Sartain.

"I do . . . opportunity": *Records*, 142.

Location: oil on canvas, unfinished: Pennsylvania Academy of the Fine Arts, Gift of Horace Howard Furness, 1899 (1899.8; 45¾" x 36 3/16", dated ca. 1867; see <https://www.pafa.org/collection/ralph-waldo-emerson> [accessed 16 August 2015]).

1866

Bas-relief of Emerson in 1866 by Charles Akers

"life-size": "Personal Glimpses of Our New England Poets. From an Artist's Autobiography," *New England Magazine* 17 (December 1897): 446, image 455.

Akers arrived . . . stay: *L*, 5:473; *LetETE*, 1:392–393.

"Mr. Emerson . . . back": "Personal Glimpses," 451.

Location: unknown.

1868

Emerson in 1868 by John Notman and Frank Rowell

FIRST SITTING

IMAGES (A)–(C)

According to . . . Boston": photocopy in the CFPL Photofile from an unlocated original.

John Sloan Notman . . . 1866: Roger Hall, *The World of William Notman: The Nineteenth Century Through a Master Lens* (Boston: David R. Godine, 1993), 38–39.

His brother . . . (1832–1900): Hall, 39.

John Notman . . . Canada: Hall, 39; Steele and Polito, 103.

Nevertheless, the . . . observed: Steele and Polito, 104, 115.

1855, for example: *American Heritage* 38.5 (July/August 1987), 107.

1865 . . . image [B]): HNE.

Photographers Allen . . . 1892: Steele and Polito, 23.

Sanborn reproduced . . . Rowell": "Portraits," 461.

"Pd Notman . . . Ellen 5.00": "Account Book 1865–1872," HL, MS Am 1280H (112g).

"Pd Notman . . . L. E. 5": "Account Book 1865–1872," HL, MS Am 1280H (112g).

"I do . . . figure": *L*, 9:330.

Locations: (A) CFPL (Newton-Emerson Collection, *Works* (Riverside Edition), vol. 10, part 2; cabinet-size paper print), JM (CDV 12; b: blank); (B) HNE (cabinet: f: Frank Rowell, 25 Winter Street; b: Allen & Rowell, 25 Winter Street); (C) Athenæum (AA.5.4.Eme.r., no. 8; cabinet: b: Edw. L. Allen and Frank Rowell, 25 Winter Street), National Portrait Gallery, London (NPG.78.6; albumen silver print attributed to Allen and Rowell Studio; b: unknown).

SECOND SITTING

IMAGES (D)–(F)

Hall reproduces . . . 1868: *World of William Notman*, 197.

"an unidentified . . . 1868: *World of William Notman*, 198.

Childs was . . . 1891: Steele and Polito, 159.

Locations: (D) Athenæum (AA.5.4.Eme.r.1867; cabinet: f: John S. Notman; b: J. Ward & Son, 125 Washington Street; Ward is listed as a photographic retailer and publisher at this address between ca. 1860–1875 [Steele and Polito, 163]), Bostonian (NEG4983; cabinet: f: John S. Notman; b: J. Ward & Son, 125 Washington Street; dated 1868); (E) JM (cabinet 10; b: blank); (F) Athenæum (photo.AA.5.4.Eme.r.no. 6; cabinet: f&b: blank), George Eastman Museum, Rochester, N.Y. (1981:3027:0005; dated by hand on back: "About 1869–70").

1868[?]

Emerson in 1868[?] by Augustus Marshall

Augustus Marshall . . . 1882: Steele and Polito, 93.

Location: JM (CDV 21; b: "MARSHALL, | Photographer, Studio Building, Cor. Tremont and Bromfield Sts. | BOSTON").

1868

Emerson with his grandson Ralph Emerson Forbes in 1868

John A. Whipple . . . 1865: *Encyclopedia of Nineteenth-Century Photography*, ed. John Hannavy (New York: Routledge, 2008), 1495.

Image (B1) . . . 1868: *LetETE*, 1:487.

"photographic head": see *JMN*, 16:377; see also 365, 378 for reference to a "photograph" of him.

"From a photograph by Marshall": "Portraits," 459.

"From a photograph . . . 1868": *W*, 8: frontispiece, [xvii].

"From a . . . *Boston: Bookman* (London) 24 (June 1903): 89.

Locations: (A) CFPL (CDV: f: Whipple, 297 Washington Street, Boston; b: blank), MHS

(Emerson Family Photographs #152.94; CDV: b: Whipple, 297 Washington Street, dated 30 May 1868); (B) CFPL (CDV-size paper print); (C) George Eastman Museum, Rochester, N.Y. (1981.3027.0001; CDV: f: Whipple, 297 Washington Street, Boston; b: blank); (D1) original: unknown; (D2) original: unknown.

Note: A hand-colored copy of image (A) is at JM (CDV 31 TK), but pasted to a sheet so the back is not visible:

1871

Emerson in 1871 by William Shew

Emerson traveled . . . 15–19 May: von Frank, 2:1022–1024.

"at the . . . photograph": *A Western Journey with Mr. Emerson* (Boston: Little, Brown, 1884), 121.

Location: JM (CDV 23).

1873

Emerson in 1873 in London by Elliott and Fry

Joseph John Elliott . . . Terrace: <www.photolondon.org.uk> (accessed 19 September 2014).

6–13 November . . . April 1873: von Frank, 2:1047, 1054–1056.

"Everyone says . . . November": *LetETE*, 2:76.

Ellen wrote . . . London: MHS, Edith Emerson Forbes and William Hathaway Forbes Papers and Additions, carton 2.

The National . . . Emerson: NPG x82283.

Image (C) is . . . *Reading: Ralph Waldo Emerson's Reading . . . with Photographs of Literary Concord . . .* (Hartford, Conn.: Transcendental Books, 1962), n.p.

Locations: (A1) Carlyle House, London (cabinet-size image mounted on board), HL, bMS Am 1280.235.706e (cabinet: f&b: Elliott & Fry, 55 and 56 Baker St.), JM (cabinet 13; b: Elliott & Fry, 55 and 56 Baker St., "Copies of this picture may always be obtained from Hegger, 152 Broadway, New York"), JM (cabinet 9; f: "The Late Ralph Waldo Emerson": b: Elliott & Fry, 55 Baker St., 7 Gloucester Terrace, and Hegger, 152 Broadway), MHS (Photo Coll 152.44; cabinet: f&b: Elliott & Fry, 55 Baker St.), MHS (Photo Coll 20, Box 5, folder 39; cabinet: f&b: blank); (A2) National Portrait Gallery, London (NPG x14304; CDV: f: Elliott & Fry, 55 Baker St.; b: Elliott & Fry, 55 and 56 Baker St.; dated 1869); (B) JM (cabinet 2; f: "The Late Ralph Waldo Emerson"; b: Elliott & Fry, 55 and 56 Baker St.); (C) original: unknown; (D) CFPL (CDV: f: Elliott & Fry, 55 Baker St; b: Elliott & Fry, Portman Square West), HL, bMS Am 1280.235.706a (CDV: f&b: Elliott & Fry, 55 Baker St.), JM (CDV 17; f&b: Elliott & Fry, 55 Baker St.); (E1) JM (CDV 6; b: Elliott & Fry, 55 Baker St); (E2) JM (CDV 22; f&b: Elliott & Fry, 55 Baker St.), National Portrait Gallery, London (2 copies: NPG x3680 and NPG Ax18267; both CDV: f: Elliott & Fry; b: Elliott & Fry, 55 Baker St.; dated 1869).

Note: Ellen wrote Elliott on 23 December 1873 that the "two dozen photographs I asked for have arrived, and I am much obliged to you for them" (JM).

1873

Emerson in 1873 by Eliphalet J. Foss

Eliphalet J. Foss . . . Massachusetts: Steele and Polito, 61, 334–335.

"My Foss . . . Chamberlaine": *JMN*, 16:462.

"~~Photographs at Foss's~~": *JMN*, 16:463.

"His return . . . ten": "Portraits," 462.

"When the . . . well": Rusk's notes.

Horatio G. Smith . . . 1909: Steele and Polito, 122.

"taken about 1873": Ireland, *Ralph Waldo Emerson*, x.

"given to . . . lately": HNE.

Emerson's *Poems*: (Boston: Houghton, Mifflin, 1884).

Charles Pollock . . . 1892: Steele and Polito, 161.

Locations: (A) Athenæum (7863A; cabinet: f&b: blank), HNE (cabinet: f&b: blank), HNE (cabinet: f: Foss, 171½ Tremont Street; b: blank); (B) Athenæum (AA.5.4.Eme.r., no. 7; cabinet: f&b: blank), Bostonian (cabinet-size paper print), CFPL (2 copies: both cabinet: b: "H. G. Smith, Studio Building, Boston"), JM (cabinet 3; f&b: blank), JM (cabinet 25; f&b: Foss's "Garden Studio," Florence St., Malden); (C) JM (cabinet 8; f: "Chas. Pollock, 2 Hamilton Place, Boston"; b: blank); (D) JM (cabinet 26; f&b: William Notman, Montreal, Toronto, Halifax"), JM (CDV 2; f&b: blank); (E) JM (cabinet 31; b: "Copyright, Charles Taber & Co., New Bedford, Mass., 1882").

1873 OR 1874

Bust of Emerson in 1873 or 1874 by Martin Milmore

Robert Lewis . . . *Homes*: [George B. Bartlett], "Ralph Waldo Emerson," Arthur Gilman et al., *Poets' Homes. Pen and Pencil Sketches of American Poets and Their Homes* (Boston: D. Lothrop, 1879), 161, and see *Note two* below.

"surprisingly good . . . sight": *L*, 228.

"I have . . . years": *L*, 6:184.

"went to . . . begged'": *LetETE*, 1:641.

"asking an . . . serene": *L*, 6:184.

"greatly esteemed": *New York Times*, 22 July 1883, 2.

Indeed, the . . . event: (Boston: Alfred Mudge, 1874), 58.

"Mr. Martin . . . Boston": 4 October 1877, 2.

Daniel Chester . . . Boston: "Daniel French Dies; Famous Sculptor," *New York Times*, 8 October 1931, 22.

Location: unknown.

Note one: The Catalogue of American Portraits from the National Portrait Gallery dates Milmore's bust 1878, describes it as "Plaster (Painted)" measuring 25 3/16" x 13 9/16" x 10 7/16", and states it was acquired in 1985 by Richard K. Dowd (VA990004).

Note two: Although the chapter on Emerson in *Poets' Homes* is usually ascribed to Richard Henry Stoddard, a notice of its original unsigned appearance in *Wide Awake* 8 (January 1879): 58–65, that appeared in the 21 December 1878 *Library Table* lists Bartlett as the author, and Lewis is credited with the drawing of Milmore's bust, with the latter attribution not carried over to the book publication, which does, however, list Appleton as the bust's owner (4:542).

MID-1870S

Emerson in the mid-1870s by George Kendall Warren

George Kendall . . . 1882: Steele and Polito, 133.

"Just added": *Bookseller* (London) no. 302 (5 January 1883): 64.

Image (B) . . . image: *Ralph Waldo Emerson's Reading . . . with Photographs of Literary Concord . . .* (Hartford, Conn.: Transcendental Books, 1962), n.p.

Locations: (A1) JM (cabinet 18; oval image; f&b: blank); (A2) Athenæum (cabinet: f&b: blank), BPL (MS2142.VII.c, no. 3; cabinet: f&b: blank), CFPL (mounted albumin print; f&b: blank), HNE (cabinet: f: Warren, 465 Washington Street; b: blank),

JM (cabinet 16; unmounted image in envelope for Notman Photographic Co., Boston and Cambridge), JM (cabinet 17; f&b: blank), JM (cabinet 19; f: Warren's; b: Warren's Portraits, 465 Washington Street, Boston), JM (cabinet 6: f: "Marton, 220 North Center, Bloomington, Illinois"; b: blank); (A3) CFPL (cabinet: f&b: blank), JM (cabinet 28; f: Bruckmann's Collection, Geo. Kirchner & Co., New York; b: blank); (B) original: unknown; (C) Athenæum (*2008.32.no. 3; cabinet: f&b: blank), New York Public Library, Prints Collection (cabinet: f: Warren's; b: Warren's Portraits, 465 Washington Street, Boston).

Note one: There is also a cabinet card with a retouched image, noted on the front as published by H. K. Saunders and copyrighted 1882:

Locations: CFPL (cabinet: f&b: blank), JM (cabinet 11; f&b: blank).

Note two: The Concord and Rhode Island artist Stacy Tolman (1860–1935) drew a crayon portrait of Emerson based on image (A1); see Leslie Perrin Wilson, "'The Tenant is More Than the House': Selected Emerson Portraits in the Concord Free Public Library," *Nineteenth-Century Prose* 33 (Spring 2006): 107–108, which reproduces the portrait on 106.

1875

Emerson, Samuel Bradford, and William Henry Furness in 1875 by Frederick Gutekunst

Frederick Gutekunst . . . leaders: Keith F. Davis, *The Origins of American Photography, from Daguerreotype to Dry-Plate, 1839–1885* (Kansas City: Hall Family Foundation in association with The Nelson-Atkins Museum of Art, Distributed by Yale University Press, 2007), 175.

From 1866 . . . Street: the address printed on the reverse of his Emerson cabinet cards.

"Father shows . . . them": *LetETE*, 2:169.

[Y]ou will . . . enlarged": *Records of a Lifelong Friendship, 1807–1882: Ralph Waldo Emerson and William Henry Furness*, ed. H[orace]. H[oward]. F[urness] (Boston: Houghton Mifflin, 1910), 165–166.

Two of . . . [c]): *Records*, facing 165, 166.

Image (B1) . . . "Portraits": 462.

"photograph of . . . ones": *LetETE*, 2:171.

"The photographs . . . choose": *L*, 10:157–158.

"It was . . . match!": *Records*, xi.

"The Emerson . . . Gutekunst": "Portraits," 463.

"Ralph Waldo . . . Gutekunst": JM.

Locations: (A1) MHS (Photo Coll 152.43; cabinet: f: blank; b: "F. Gutekunst, 712 Arch Street, Philadelphia"); (A2) original: unknown; (B1) JM (cabinet 29; f: embossed Gutekunst logo; b: blank); (B2) JM (cabinet 21; f: F. Gutekunst, Philadelphia; b: "F. Gutekunst, 712 Arch Street, Philadelphia"); (c) CFPL (cabinet: f: blank; b: "F. Gutekunst, 712 Arch Street, Philadelphia"); (D) CFPL (cabinet: f: blank; b: "F. Gutekunst, 712 Arch Street, Philadelphia"), National Portrait Gallery, Washington, D.C. (77.171; cabinet: f: F. Gutekunst, Philadelphia; b: partially abraded with Gutekunst and Philadelphia partially legible but not the street address).

1876

Edward Waldo Emerson and Emerson holding Charles Lowell Emerson in 1876

Image (A) . . . son: 2:238–240.

"Paid Whipple, . . . 17.00": "Account Book 1872–1882," HL, MS Am 1280H (112h).

Locations: (A) CFPL (cabinet-size paper print), JM (cabinet 5; f: blank; b: "Successors to Whipple[,] Metcalfe & Welldon, 24 Temple Place, Boston"); (B) JM (cabinet 4; b: unknown).

LATE 1870S

Emerson in the late 1870s by George Kendall Warren

Warren was . . . 1882: Steele and Polito, 133.

These may . . . 1879: Rusk's notes.

Locations: (A) JM (cabinet 15); (B) JM (cabinet 24).

1878

Sketch of Emerson in July 1878 by Wyatt Eaton

"it had . . . clear": "Recollections of American Poets," *Century Magazine* 64 (October 1902): 842–850.

Ellen Emerson . . . 1872–1873: *LetETE*, 2:307.

"used to . . . paper": "Portraits," 463.

"these pleasant . . . seen": "Portraits," 466–467.

"I will . . . *effigies*": "Portraits," 462.

Location: Huntington Library, Art Collections, and Botanical Gardens (81.11.1HL; graphite on paper; 18¼" x 14").

Note one: Timothy Cole engraved this image as the frontispiece of the February 1879 *Scribner's Monthly* in connection with Sanborn's "The Home and Haunts of Emerson" in that issue:

The image was reprinted in Sanborn's "Ralph Waldo Emerson" in *The Homes and Haunts of Our Elder Poets* and, again by Sanborn, in "Portraits" (17: 496–511; [New York: D. Appleton, 1881], after 30; "Portraits," 464).

Note two: Neither of the two copies of Herrick's poems now in Emerson's library contains a picture of the author, but he may have used an unlocated edition with one of the popular images of Herrick, such as this one:

See Walter Harding, *Emerson's Library* (Charlottesville: University Press of Virginia, 1967), 134, for editions of Herrick owned by Emerson.

1879

Emerson in his study in 1879 by Augustus H. Folsom

Augustus H. Folsom . . . 1879: Steele and Polito, 421.

in 1889 . . . 1843: *Cuttyhunk and the Elizabeth Islands*, ed. Cuttyhunk Historical Society (Charleston, S.C.: Arcadia, 2002), 213.

Location: HL, (pf) Autograph File, Folsom, A. H. (image size 6" x 8" with printed A. H. Folsom, 48 Alleghany Street, Roxbury; mounted on stiff paper board with "October 1879 R W E in his Study" written on back).

1879

Bust of Emerson in 1879 by Daniel Chester French

IMAGES (A)–(C)

In 1876 . . . Road: Michael Richman, *Daniel Chester French: An American Sculptor* (New York: Metropolitan Museum of Art for the National Trust for Historic Preservation, 1976), 4; Concord Historical Commission, *Historical and Architectural Resources, Concord, Massachusetts*, 4 vols. (Concord: The Commission, 1994), 3:206.

Also in . . . $30.00: Richman, 51, 52.

"Dan, that's . . . shave": Margaret French Cresson, *Journey into Fame: The Life of Daniel Chester French* (Cambridge, Mass.: Harvard University Press, 1947), 121.

"I wonder . . . satisfactory'": *LetETE*, 2:345–346, which reproduces on 346 the bust as it appeared in the front sitting room of Bush.

"almost child-like . . . sought": *A Memoir of Ralph Waldo Emerson*, 2 vols. (Boston: Houghton, Mifflin, 1887), 2:678–679.

"a gift . . . contributor": "Report of the Trustees of the Free Public Library," *Annual Reports of the Selectmen and Other Officers of the Town of Concord, From March 1st, 1883, to March 1st, 1884, Being the Two Hundred and Forty-Eighth Municipal Year* (Boston: Tolman & White, 1884), 52.

Locations: plaster: (A) Art Institute of Chicago, Bush (22" high), CFPL (2 copies, both 23"); marble: (B) CFPL (24½"); (C) Harvard University Portrait Collection; 23⅝"; Gift of Henry Lee and Henry L. Higginson to Harvard College, 1883.

Note one: A picture of the plaster bust served as the frontispiece to *W*, 12, where it is incorrectly dated "1878":

Note two: A copy of the bust measuring 20½" high and described as "Green patinated plaster, made to look like weathered bronze," is at the New-York Historical Society, the gift of French's daughter, Margaret French Cresson (1953.15).

Note three: By 1886, bronze copies of the Emerson bust were also available for sale. The piece—which French had copyrighted in August 1879—was one of the sculptor's dependable money-makers.

Courtesy Concord Museum

For more on the variations among the different busts, see Richman, 51–54, and Richman, "Daniel Chester French," *Metamorphoses in Nineteenth-Century Sculpture*, ed. Jeanne L. Wasserman (Cambridge, Mass.: Fogg Art Museum, Harvard University Press, 1975), 224–239.

Locations: Concord Museum (2013.011AB; cast about 1905; 21¾" high; gift of William T. Loomis and Leslie Becker, 2013), Metropolitan Museum of Art (07.101; 22½"; gift of the artist, 1907 and cast 1906–1907).

1879

Emerson and his extended family in 1879

IMAGE (A)

"Standing, from . . . Charles: *LetETE*, 2:369, cropped without the date.

Rusk identifies . . . Folsom: Rusk's notes.

"two days . . . dead": Charles Duffy, "Material Relating to R. W. Emerson in the Grimm *Nachlass*," *American Literature* 30 (January 1959): 524–525.

Location: CFPL (paper print; 4¾" x 6¾").

IMAGE (B)

Location: MHS (Edith Emerson Forbes scrapbook, 1860–1920, Edith Emerson Forbes and William Hathaway Forbes Papers and Additons, Carton 26, Barcode SH 17QA 3, Folder 21).

EARLY 1880S

Emerson in the early 1880s by George Kendall Warren

Warren was . . . 1882: Steele and Polito, 133.

Locations: JM (cabinet 22; f: blank; b: covered with pasted labels), JM (cabinet 27; f: Warren's; b: Warren's Portraits).

EARLY 1880S

Emerson in the early 1880s

Locations: (A) JM (cabinet 12; f&b: blank), Lincoln Financial Foundation Collection, Allen County Public Library, Fort Wayne, Indiana (LN-0524; cabinet: f&b: blank); (B) Athenæum (1803.1882; cabinet-size paper print: b: unknown [image pasted down]); (C) JM (cabinet 14; f&b: blank).

Note: Image (C) may be the one to which Ellen Emerson referred when she wrote her sister Edith on 13 February 1879, "Don't you think that least distinct picture of Father reading his newspaper was good? I did" (*LetETE*, 2:334). If so, then these images should be dated "1879."

EARLY 1880S

Emerson in the early 1880s by George Kendall Warren

Warren was . . . 1882: Steele and Polito, 133.

Locations: HL, bMS Am 1280.235.706d (cabinet), JM (cabinet 23).

APPENDIX A: APOCRYPHAL IMAGES OF EMERSON

1837

Silhouette and watercolor by Thomas Edwards

Reproduced in . . . 5¾": *The American Heritage Auction of Americana*, Sotheby Parke Bernet, New York, auction 4048, 17–19 November 1977, lot 692.

Audubon and his wife: reproduced in the same catalogue as lot 625.

descriptions of Emerson lecturing: see John Townsend Trowbridge, *My Own Story, With Recollections of Noted Persons* (Boston: Houghton Mifflin, 1903), 348.

signature is . . . Edwards: see lots 626, 693, and 694 for comparison.

1841[?]

Drawing in 1841[?] by "W. M. T."

No notes.

1847

Engraving in 1847 by Henry Clark Pidgeon

On 2 September . . . declined: *L*, 3:417–418.

"I saw . . . feared": Elizabeth Maxfield-Miller, "Elizabeth of Concord: Selected Letters of Elizabeth Sherman Hoar (1814–1878) to the Emersons, Family, and the Emerson Circle (Part Three)," *Studies in the American Renaissance 1986*, ed. Joel Myerson (Charlottesville: University Press of Virginia, 1986), 159.

"never seen . . . mention": *L*, 4:16.

"In due . . . face": 2 (11 December 1847): 369–371; image on 369 with the artist's information, quote on 470.

"We present . . . likeness": "Ralph Waldo Emerson," 2:32.

Another version . . . *Orations*: (London: Ingram Cook, 1853).

1857

Bas-relief in 1857 by Joseph Carew

"was quite . . . life": William Reese, Art Bulletin 6, item 4.

In 1857 . . . Common: *The Boston Almanac for the Year 1857* (Boston: John P. Jewett, 1856), 140.

Location: Brick Row Bookshop, San Francisco (marble; 20½" x 15").

1857

Oliver Wendell Holmes and Emerson[?] in the Boston Public Garden in 1857

"The Beacon . . . Conversation": (Boston: Houghton Mifflin, 1915), facing 142, and credited to the Boston Athenæum.

Location: Athenæum (photo A B64B6 P.g. [no.1]; 4½" x 7").

LATE 1850S

Emerson in the late 1850s attributed to Mathew Brady

"Emerson at . . . 1859": (Berkeley: University of California Press, 1995), following 336.

Richardson has . . . 1860s": Richardson's carte-de-visite and the clipped catalogue entry are at CFPL.

E. Anthony of 501 Broadway: JM (CDV 14).

Cedric L. Robinson . . . cartes-de-visite": Keith F. Davis, *The Origins of American Photography, from Daguerreotype to Dry-Plate, 1839–1885* (Kansas City: Hall Family Foundation in association with The Nelson-Atkins Museum of Art, Distributed by Yale University Press, 2007), 86; Beaumont Newhall, *The History of Photography, from 1839 to the Present Day*, 4th ed. (New York: Museum of Modern Art, 1964), 26.

Historical Portraits: 28 vols. (New York: privately printed, 1913–1915); the present image appears on 1:62.

Meserve's Brady . . . by Brady: Jay Pridmore, "Famous Were Photographer Brady's Bunch," *Chicago Tribune*, 29 September 1995; see *Historical Portraits*, 1:62–64 and 21:44–45.

BEFORE 1862

Undated silhouette

Portraits and . . . Authors: (Boston: Houghton, Mifflin, 1893).

Location: Concord Museum (1991.009; 8¾" x 10¾").

1874[?]

Bust of Emerson in 1874[?] by John Crookshanks King

"modelled in 1854": 42:429.

Born in . . . died: Lorado Taft, *History of American Sculpture* (New York: Macmillan, 1903), 94.

Emerson wrote a letter: *L*, 5:89–90.

King's busts of Samuel Hoar and Daniel Webster: the former now at CFPL.

Catalogue of Oil-Paintings . . . 1874: (Boston: Rand, Avery, 1874).

"unspeakably bad": "Portraits," 468.

Location: unknown.

Note one: *Catalogue of . . . Brother*: (Boston: P. P. Caproni and Brother, 1913), 54.

Note two: "It looks . . . parsnip": *Ralph Waldo Emerson: Days of Encounter* (Boston: Little, Brown, 1984), 422–423 (no source cited).

"made at . . . parsnip'": "The Emerson Statue by Daniel C. French, Sculptor," *International Studio* 53.211 (September 1914): lxi.

"another bust . . . parsnip'": "A Sculptor's Reminiscences of Emerson," *Art World* 1.1 (October 1916): 44, 47.

Note three: Among the many parian busts of "Emerson" is this undated, unsigned one at JM:

However, this is clearly a variant of the bust of Emerson made by Robinson and Leadbeater, Stoke-on-Trent, England, that has been featured in numerous auctions. The busts range in size from 7½" to 13¾" and are usually dated as late nineteenth-century.

1900[?]

Bust of Emerson in 1900[?] by Sidney H. Morse

The Second . . . Boston: The Second Church in Boston: Commemorative Services Held on the Completion of Two Hundred and Fifty Years Since Its Foundation, 1649–1899 (Boston: The Society, 1900), facing 46.

"While [the . . . discarded": TLS, CFPL Photofile E, "Emerson, R. W., Busts of."

William Taylor Newton's *Emersoniana: Vol. XIII, 1904–1905*, now part of the Newton/Emerson Collection at CFPL.

original photograph by Baldwin Coolidge: HNE.

"Morse's reduced . . . it": "Portraits," 468.

N.D.

Undated painting

"Portrait of . . . Emerson": (New York: Viking, 1996), credited to The Metropolitan Museum of Art, New York (Bequest of Chester Dale, 1962).

Life in America (New York: Metropolitan Museum of Art, 1939), 77 (picture), 78.

Location: The Metropolitan Museum of Art, New York (64.974; 20½" x 15½"; <http://www.metmuseum.org/collection/the-collection-online/search/12994?rpp=30&pg=1&ft=chester+dale&pos=6> [accessed 18 August 2015]).

APPENDIX B: UNLOCATED IMAGES OF EMERSON

1848

"M. Lehmann . . . head": *JMN*, 10:277.

"The artists . . . type": *JMN*, 10:434.

"made a . . . writer": Ireland, 55.

1852

Caroline Davis Wilson . . . bust of him: *L*, 4:330.

July 1852 . . . Concord: *L*, 4:330n.

mid-August: Henry David Thoreau walked to Fair Haven Hill with her and her son on 12 August (*Journal, Volume 5:1852–1853*, ed. Patrick F. O'Connell [Princeton: Princeton University Press, 1997], 295).

"Mrs Wilson . . . bust": *L*, 4:333.

"daily": *L*, 4:333.

In June 1853 . . . him: *L*, 8:370.

May-Day: *JMN*, 16:59.

"stopped the . . . 1852: *Artists in Ohio, 1787–1900: A Biographical Dictionary* ed. Mary Sayre Haverstock (Kent, Ohio: Kent State University Press, 2000), 952.

Emerson did . . . sculpture: *JMN*, 11:516.

1855

"photographic likeness . . . men": 2, Rusk's notes.

1858

"Father is . . . 'swinish-looking'": *LetETE*, 1:141–142.

"studio was . . . canvases": William Ward Wight, *The Wights: A Record of Thomas Wight of Dedham and Medfield and of his Descendants 1635–1890* (Milwaukee: Swain & Tate, 1890), 191.

1866

"stay for . . . morning": *L*, 5:486; text from a sales catalogue.

1868

"a little . . . good": *LetETE*, 1:464–465.

"Where are Father's tin-types?": *LetETE*, 1:469.

1873

"large Robert . . . considerably aged": Rusk's notes.

Emerson had . . . 1848 : *JMN*, 10:219–220.

1879

"October of . . . path": Charles Duffy, "Material Relating to R. W. Emerson in the Grimm *Nachlass*," *American Literature* 30 (January 1959): 524–525.

Index

This index contains proper names mentioned in the text and libraries which possess images of Emerson. We have not indexed the proper names of recipients of letters. Page numbers for images reproduced in main entries (in the text and the notes) are in italics, as are those for reproductions of selected secondary images.

Contributors

Joel Myerson, Carolina Distinguished Professor of American Literature, Emeritus, has written or edited some sixty books on Emerson and the Transcendentalists, most recently (with Ronald A. Bosco), *Ralph Waldo Emerson: The Major Prose* (Harvard). In August 2016, he and Bosco jointly received the Julian P. Boyd Award, the highest award presented by the Association for Documentary Editing, given every three years to a senior scholar in honor of a distinguished contribution to the study of American history and culture.

Leslie Perrin Wilson is Curator of the William Munroe Special Collections at the Concord (Massachusetts) Free Public Library, a repository known for significant holdings of photographs and works of art depicting Emerson. She has written extensively on local historical and literary topics—Emerson portraiture included—for scholarly and general audiences. Her book *In History's Embrace* appeared in 2007, her all-new guidebook section for the history-cum-tourist guide *Historic Concord and the Lexington Fight* in 2010 (updated printing 2016). Her most recently published exhibition catalog, *From* Thoreau's Seasons *to* Men of Concord: *N. C. Wyeth Inspired*, appeared in April 2016.